How Should Society Respond to the Refugee Crisis?

Other titles in the *Issues Today* series include:

How Can Gun Violence Be Stopped?
How Does Fake News Threaten Society?
How Should America Deal with Undocumented Immigrants?
How Should Extremist Content Be Regulated on Social Media?
What Are the Dangers of Online Scams?
How Has the #MeToo Movement Changed Society?

ISSUES TODAY

How Should Society Respond to the Refugee Crisis?

Stephanie Lundquist-Arora

San Diego, CA

© 2021 ReferencePoint Press, Inc.
Printed in the United States

For more information, contact:
ReferencePoint Press, Inc.
PO Box 27779
San Diego, CA 92198
www.ReferencePointPress.com

ALL RIGHTS RESERVED.
No part of this work covered by the copyright hereon may be reproduced or used in any form or by any means—graphic, electronic, or mechanical, including photocopying, recording, taping, web distribution, or information storage retrieval systems—without the written permission of the publisher.

LIBRARY OF CONGRESS CATALOGING-IN-PUBLICATION DATA

Names: Lundquist-Arora, Stephanie, author.
Title: How should society respond to the refugee crisis? / by Stephanie
   Lundquist-Arora.
Description: San Diego, CA : ReferencePoint Press, Inc., 2021. | Series:
   Issues today | Includes bibliographical references and index.
Identifiers: LCCN 2019051366 (print) | LCCN 2019051367 (ebook) | ISBN
   9781682828854 (library binding) | ISBN 9781682828861 (ebook)
Subjects: LCSH: Refugees--Government policy. | Refugees.
Classification: LCC HV640 .L85 2021 (print) | LCC HV640 (ebook) | DDC
   362.87/56--dc23
LC record available at https://lccn.loc.gov/2019051366
LC ebook record available at https://lccn.loc.gov/2019051367

CONTENTS

Introduction   6
A Global Crisis

Chapter One   10
Who Are the Refugees?

Chapter Two   21
The Perilous Journey

Chapter Three   31
Hurdles and Outcomes for Refugee Status

Chapter Four   43
The US Response

Chapter Five   53
In Search of a Global Solution

Source Notes   65
Organizations and Websites   70
For Further Research   72
Index   73
Picture Credits   79
About the Author   80

INTRODUCTION

A Global Crisis

Twelve-year-old Jasmine and her mother and sisters are living in a small tent in a camp near the Syrian border. Jasmine is not going to school. She helps take care of her younger sisters when their mother leaves for the day to find work and food in nearby towns. They had to leave their home because it was not safe. During the ongoing war in Syria, bombs destroyed all but one room of their house. For two weeks, they all lived in that one room. Then Jasmine's father was shot in front of his family. During the civil war in Syria, men and teenage boys are sometimes rounded up and killed for fear that they are fighting with the opposing side. Jasmine explains what she witnessed: "My father left the room. I watched my father leave, and watched as my father was shot outside our home. I started to cry, I was so sad. We were living a normal life. We had enough food, now we depend on others. Everything changed for me that day."[1]

Refugee Numbers Are Growing

There are many stories like Jasmine's, particularly in Syria. Since the civil war began in 2011, an estimated five hundred thousand people have been killed. Many Syrians have fled and are looking for safety. According to the United Nations High Commissioner for Refugees (UNHCR), since the beginning of the war, more than 5.5 million Syrians have become refugees. As large a number as this is, it represents only a fraction of the refugees worldwide.

There are 25.9 million refugees worldwide. More than half of them are children. They come from many places. Most come from Syria, Afghanistan, South Sudan, Myanmar, Somalia, Sudan, and the Democratic Republic of the Congo. They risk their lives on perilous journeys to find safety as they encounter warring groups of soldiers, human traffickers, and people who exploit their tragedies for profit. For example, malicious entrepreneurs have charged large sums of money for fake life jackets that do not float. Refugees have bought these life jackets before boarding overcrowded fishing vessels—not knowing that the jackets will be useless if the boat capsizes on its voyage across the ocean. In other cases, refugees have been captured by human traffickers and sold as slaves in the sex trade.

"I watched . . . as my father was shot outside our home. I started to cry, I was so sad. We were living a normal life. We had enough food, now we depend on others. Everything changed for me that day."[1]

—Jasmine, a twelve-year-old Syrian refugee

The number of people forcibly displaced has doubled in the past twenty years. The growth rate of displaced people is increasing more quickly than the ability (or will) of the global community to address the problem. The UNHCR estimates that in 2018, less

Refugees from the war in Syria wait to board a train that will transport them to safe haven in Germany. Worldwide, there are more than 25 million refugees, more than half of them children.

than 7 percent of refugees were resettled. The remaining refugees find themselves in refugee camps, usually in their country of origin at first, and then across a nearby border.

Refugee camps are not all the same. People may live in tents, under tarps, in shipping containers, or in concrete buildings. Services and care also vary greatly. Settlements that are run by the United Nations (UN) have more resources, such as schools and health care, but other settlements consist of makeshift camps outside of cities and have little support. Some people stay there for weeks and others for years. The average stay in a resettlement camp worldwide is seventeen years. Some families remain in the same camp for multiple generations.

Disagreement Stymies Response

Many people believe that more should be done to help refugees. Data from the Pew Research Center suggest that people are more generous in granting resettlement for refugees than they are for immigrants in general. "Across the 18 countries surveyed," a 2019 Pew report noted, "a median of 71% of adults said they support taking in refugees fleeing violence and war."[2] Meanwhile, a median of 50 percent of respondents said they support taking in more or about the same number of immigrants.

Despite these views, the world's nations do not agree on how to respond. Refugee resettlement efforts are often stymied by arguments over who should do what and for whom. There are debates over security. Some countries worry that people posing as refugees might be terrorists. Other debates revolve around the costs that will be borne by host countries. There are large populations of people who do not speak the language of the host country and need houses, food, jobs, education, and health care. While there

> "Across the 18 countries surveyed, a median of 71% of adults said they support taking in refugees fleeing violence and war."[2]
>
> —Raea Rasmussen and Jacob Poushter, researchers at the Pew Research Center

appears to be support for taking in refugees, the debates over logistical matters cause delay or inaction.

All of these considerations influence policy at the domestic level in host countries. In recent years the United States in particular has significantly decreased the number of refugees allowed to enter the country. From 1980 until 2018, the United States resettled more refugees than any other country in the world. However, US refugee resettlement dropped from 97,000 in 2016 to a proposed 18,000 in 2020. The decrease of refugee resettlement in the United States has led to an increased number of refugee applications, and sometimes resettlements, in other host countries. Because the US resettlement of refugees was a significant portion of total resettlement worldwide, US president Donald Trump's administration's changes to refugee policy in the United States have dramatically affected overall worldwide resettlement numbers. Globally, there were 189,000 refugee resettlements in 2016, but the number fell to 92,000 in 2018.

Some people argue that the United States should increase its refugee resettlements to help resolve the crisis. Others suggest that a global crisis needs a global solution and that other countries need to do more as well. The questions of who should bear the responsibility and who should get priority are highly contentious. However, a large displaced population—over half of them children—living in difficult conditions (and sometimes dying in transit) constitutes a global humanitarian crisis that deserves attention.

CHAPTER ONE

Who Are the Refugees?

Malala Yousafzai was eleven years old when she fled Pakistan with her family. The Taliban, a militant Islamic fundamentalist group, had prohibited the education of girls and subsequently destroyed many of the girls' schools in Pakistan and neighboring Afghanistan. The Taliban required girls and women to cover their faces in public and banned children's games and music devices. They ruled by fear and lined the streets with the dead bodies of the people who spoke out against them. Pakistan's and Afghanistan's armies launched military operations to fight the Taliban. Many civilians, including Yousafzai's cousin, were shot in the cross fire between them. No one felt safe. Yousafzai, who now lives in the United Kingdom, explains, "At night, my family and I would sometimes huddle on the floor, as far away from the windows as possible, as we heard bombs exploding and the rat-a-tat of machine guns in the hills surrounding Mingora."[3]

Yousafzai's life was not always plagued by violence and worries. She has memories of happier times before the arrival of the Taliban. Her childhood memories include family picnics and "running in the streets with my friends; playing on the roof of our house in Mingora; visiting our cousins and extended family in Shangla; listening to my mother and

> "At night, my family and I would sometimes huddle on the floor, as far away from the windows as possible, as we heard bombs exploding and the rat-a-tat of machine guns in the hills surrounding Mingora."[3]
>
> —Malala Yousafzai, Pakistani refugee and winner of the 2014 Nobel Peace Prize

all her friends chatting over afternoon tea in our home, and my father discussing politics with friends."[4]

Despite the ongoing violence and restrictions of Taliban rule, the Yousafzai family had returned to the Swat Valley. After their return, Malala Yousafzai began advocating publicly for educational rights for girls, which made her a target for the Taliban. In October 2012 a masked gunman boarded her school bus and shot her in the left side of the head. She survived the attack and woke up ten days later in a hospital in England. After months of multiple surgeries and

At just eleven years old, Malala Yousafzai (pictured) was shot in retaliation for speaking out against attempts by the repressive Taliban regime to deny education to girls in her native Pakistan. She and her family escaped to the West, where she continues to advocate for education.

rehabilitation, Yousafzai reunited with her family in their new home in the United Kingdom.

When the Yousafzais left Pakistan for the last time, their lives were in imminent danger. They joined millions of other refugees—all with the same hope of finding safety for themselves and their families.

The number of refugees under the UNHCR mandate has nearly doubled since 2012, as refugees have streamed out of countries devastated by violence. Some experts contend that the refugee situation has escalated to a global crisis. David Miliband, chief executive officer of the International Rescue Committee, argues, "The rising tide of people forced to leave their homes because of conflict or persecution is one of the most challenging issues facing the world today."[5]

> "The rising tide of people forced to leave their homes because of conflict or persecution is one of the most challenging issues facing the world today."[5]
>
> —David Miliband, chief executive officer of the International Rescue Committee

Refugees and Displaced People

The UNHCR reports that by the end of 2018, more than 70.8 million people, which is roughly the population of California and Texas combined, have had to leave their homes because of persecution, conflict, or violence. About 13.6 million of them left their homes during 2018. A little over a third of the forcibly displaced, 25.9 million people, are classified as refugees. The UN 1951 Convention Relating to the Status of Refugees defines a refugee as someone who,

> owing to well-founded fear of being persecuted for reasons of race, religion, nationality, membership of a particular social group or political opinion, is outside the country of his nationality and is unable or, owing to such fear, is unwilling to avail himself of the protection of that country; or who, not having a nationality and being outside the country of his former habitual residence, is unable or, owing to such fear, is unwilling to return to it.[6]

In brief, a refugee fears persecution, is outside of his or her home country, and is unable to return home.

The definition of refugee is specific and does not cover certain categories of people who are forced from their homes in times of crisis. For example, several million people are living in displacement camps in their country of origin and have not yet made it to an international border. These people are called internally displaced persons (IDPs) but are not technically refugees because they are not outside their country. IDPs are particularly vulnerable because they do not have the same rights as refugees as defined under international law. They lack the same legal standing as refugees and are often deprived of health care, education, income opportunities, food, and security. They are also at heightened risk for assault, attack, and abduction because they must

Famous Refugees

Refugees have contributed greatly to the United States throughout American history. Some have even become nationally recognized. As a German Jew in 1933, Albert Einstein fled Nazi persecution and found refuge in Princeton, New Jersey. Einstein's theory of relativity changed the face of science and even the world. His lesser-known contribution, however, is that he created the foundation for the International Rescue Committee, which continues to provide humanitarian aid to families caught in crisis worldwide.

Many American artists are also refugees. Actress Mila Kunis, who starred in the TV series *That '70s Show* and the film *Bad Moms*, arrived on a religious refugee visa from Ukraine in 1991. Kunis says, "After the Holocaust, in Russia you were not allowed to be religious, so my parents raised me to know I was Jewish. You know who you are inside." At age thirteen, rapper K'naan escaped the Somali civil war and lived as a refugee in New York for a year before reconnecting with his father in Canada. He opposes the war in Somalia through his music. Singer-songwriter Gloria Estefan and her family also fled to the United States as refugees after the Cuban Revolution.

Some influential politicians are refugees as well. Madeleine Albright, former US ambassador to the UN and the first female secretary of state, sought refuge in Denver, Colorado, in 1949. A communist coup in (then) Czechoslovakia drove her and her family from their home. Many refugees have made substantial contributions to the country in which they settle.

Quoted in Jacob Shamsian, "12 Celebrities You Didn't Realize Were Refugees," *The Independent* (London), October 22, 2017. www.independent.co.uk.

make their way through unstable areas with limited resources. Often IDPs are forced from their homes because they belong to a different ethnic group or religion than the people who wield power in their area. When they seek food and other humanitarian aid in camps within their own country, they are sitting targets for the people who drove them out of their homes. The Swiss-based Internal Displacement Monitoring Centre estimates that 41.3 million people were internally displaced worldwide at the end of 2018. Many IDPs stay in displacement camps, while others live with family members in their country of origin. IDPs' situation is difficult because it is the country of origin's responsibility to provide them with assistance and protection. In some cases though, the country of origin is persecuting them.

Ishmael Beah was once an internally displaced person. At twelve years old, he was separated from his parents and on the run for a year from Revolutionary United Front rebels in Sierra Leone, Africa. When he encountered government forces, they offered food and temporary protection to him and other young boys. It was not long, however, until these forces compelled him and the other boys to fight against the rebels. The youngest among them was a seven-year-old. Government forces gave the boys drugs, handed out automatic rifles, and pointed them toward the battleground. Many of the boys did not survive. There are ongoing conflicts around the world today that continue to use child soldiers. Many of them started out as IDPs who were separated from their families. Beah eventually made it out of Sierra Leone and settled as a refugee in the United States. Speaking at a conference when he was sixteen years old, he said, "It was not easy being a soldier, but we just had to do it. I have been rehabilitated now so don't be afraid of me. I am not a soldier anymore; I am a child."[7]

> "It was not easy being a soldier, but we just had to do it. I have been rehabilitated now so don't be afraid of me. I am not a soldier anymore; I am a child."[7]
>
> —Ishmael Beah, refugee and former child soldier from Sierra Leone

Legal Rights

According to the World Health Organization, in 2019, 258 million people were living outside their country of origin. These people are called migrants. Migrants leave their country for various reasons. Some are in search of an economic opportunity (economic migrants), but others have fled violence or persecution (displaced persons). While all refugees and displaced persons are migrants, not all migrants are displaced people or refugees. Many migrants who flee violence or persecution make it across an international border but do not have their legal documents, which prolongs the refugee application process. Without legal standing, displaced persons have limited opportunities for employment and education, and they often lack access to health care. Some economic migrants and displaced people resort to selling sex or drugs to make money for their families. Abdul, a fourteen-year-old Rohingya refugee from Myanmar at a camp in Bangladesh, says, "People in the camps are always trying to sell [methamphetamine] to me. They try to convince me that if I

Rohingya refugees from Myanmar wait for food at a refugee camp in Bangladesh. Myanmar's constitution does not recognize the Rohingya as citizens, so they have frequently been targets of persecution and forced to relocate outside the country.

sell drugs I can make money and buy more things for my family."[8] International organizations provide assistance and services to migrants in some displacement camps, but conditions vary greatly across camps.

The terms used to describe people are tied to the legal rights they receive. Refugees receive more protection under international law than do economic migrants or internally displaced persons, who have yet to cross an international border. One of the most important rights granted to refugees under the 1951 Convention Relating to the Status of Refugees is the right not to be forced to go back to their country of origin. The convention states, "No Contracting State shall expel or return . . . a refugee in any manner whatsoever to the frontiers of territories where his life or freedom would be threatened on account of his race, religion, nationality, membership of a particular social group or political opinion."[9] Other provisions from the convention specify access to courts, education, housing, and freedom of movement.

Displaced by the Holocaust

Michael Pupa's family was one of millions of Jewish families destroyed by the Holocaust. Pupa was born in Manewicz, Poland, in 1938. The Nazis killed his parents in 1942, when he was just four years old. For the next two years, Pupa was on the run with his uncle, hiding out in the forests of Poland. When the Russians liberated that part of Poland in the summer of 1944, Pupa and many others found themselves in displaced persons (DP) camps in the US-occupied part of Germany. He lived in four different DP camps for the next seven years.

After many years in DP camps, his uncle's wife died, and the uncle could no longer care for Pupa. Pupa consequently became eligible for resettlement in the United States under the priority category "Unaccompanied Displaced Child." In May 1951 the twelve-year-old Pupa flew to New York, where he lived for six months in a UN home for refugee children. He then moved to Cleveland, Ohio, where foster parents Edward and Bernice Rosenthal raised him along with their biological children. In 1957 Pupa became a citizen of the United States.

International Cooperation

International law used to determine refugee status today was created as a result of the refugee crisis during and after World War II, which lasted from 1939 to 1945. During the war, over 60 million people were killed. While 15 million of these deaths were in battle, the other 45 million were civilians. Adolf Hitler's Nazi regime tried to exterminate Europe's Jewish population, resulting in the deaths of 6 million Jews. Nazis also murdered people with disabilities, Gypsies, homosexual people, and Jehovah's Witnesses.

The Nazi persecutions of Jews and other minorities led to a global refugee crisis. An estimated 60 million Europeans became refugees during the course of the war. Many of them were orphaned children. It was a humanitarian crisis to which individual nations could not respond quickly enough. Millions of refugees were living in resettlement camps throughout Europe for several years. By 1951, six years after the war had ended, 1 million of World War II's refugees and displaced persons still had not been resettled. In response to the global crisis, in 1950 the UN created a refugee agency called the United Nations High Commissioner for Refugees. The 1951 Refugee Convention is the document that provides the mandate and framework for the UNHCR. The United States was not among the 145 member signatories of the document in 1951 but later signed its 1967 protocol, which broadened the scope of the Refugee Convention.

In the United States, President Harry Truman issued a presidential directive in 1945 to address the post–World War II refugee situation, which expedited admissions. The directive resulted in the resettlement of over forty thousand refugees and displaced persons in the United States. Truman further urged Congress to pass legislation to allow the resettlement of more refugees. He argued, "These victims of war and oppression look hopefully to the democratic countries to help them rebuild their lives and provide for the future of their children. We must not destroy their hope. The only civilized course is to enable these people to take new roots in friendly soil."[10] In 1948 the US Congress passed the Displaced Persons Act. The law allowed displaced persons and refugees to find a place to live and work in the United States. More than 350,000 refugees settled in the United States as a result.

> "These victims of war and oppression look hopefully to the democratic countries to help them rebuild their lives and provide for the future of their children. We must not destroy their hope."[10]
>
> —US president Harry Truman in 1947

Refugees Today

Today more than half of the world's refugees come from Syria, Afghanistan, and South Sudan. Other countries of origin include Myanmar, Somalia, Sudan, the Democratic Republic of the Congo, the Central African Republic, Eritrea, and Burundi. Syrians constitute the largest refugee population in the world—approximately 5.6 million as of April 2019. Syrian government and resistance forces have been fighting since 2011, and there have been many civilian casualties. The Syrian Observatory for Human Rights estimates that as of March 2018, 511,000 people have been killed in Syria. The UNHCR estimates that 6.6 million Syrians are displaced internally. Warring groups bomb schools, houses, medical facilities, and other resources, rendering cities inhospitable after a battle is over. Antigovernment militant groups have kidnapped, tortured, killed, and maimed civilians in their attacks on cities. Homemade explosive devices are planted and left to kill and injure people long after the fighting ends. In 2018 these explosives were the leading cause of child casualties in Syria, accounting for 434 deaths of children. Armed groups also interfere with humanitarian aid intended for the areas they control. The UNHCR states that "the Syrian situation is the most dramatic humanitarian crisis the world has faced in a very long time."[11]

Syrian and other refugees are going to many different countries. They are embarking on desperate journeys and trying to arrive anywhere they can find safety. Because of the cost and risks associated with their journeys, 80 percent of refugees end up living in countries that border their country of origin. For this reason, currently the world's top refugee-hosting countries include Turkey (3.7 million), Pakistan (1.4 million), Uganda (1.2 million), and Sudan (1.1 million).

More than half of the world's refugees are under eighteen years old. Many of them are traveling without their parents. Twin sixteen-year-old brothers Ibrahim and Aimamo left the Gambia, a nation in West Africa, on their own in search of economic opportunities in Italy. They made a deal with human traffickers to pay for their passage by working when they arrived in Libya. The 2017 report *Harrowing Journeys* from the United Nations Children's Fund details their experience: "Along with 200 other sub-Saharan Africans,

Source: "The World's Refugees in Numbers," Amnesty International, 2019. amnesty.org.

they spent two months working on a farm—and enduring beatings and threats. When work was done for the day, they were locked in to prevent them from escaping. After that ordeal, getting on the flimsy inflatable raft that took them to Italy was a relief."[12]

When people live in a stable place, they sometimes have a hard time believing things might not always be that way. They usually do not think too much about stopping by a market for food, visiting a doctor, going to school, or playing outside with friends. Malala Yousafzai, Ishmael Beah, and many other refugees once engaged in those kinds of activities, too. They describe a happy, normal childhood before war touched their lives. Most refugees were not always refugees. They had a reality that was different from running from danger and hoping for survival. Every refugee has a story that goes far beyond a simple legal category or statistic.

CHAPTER TWO

The Perilous Journey

On April 22, 2019, relief spotters at the Korakas lighthouse of the Greek Aegean Islands identified a small boat in the Aegean Sea several miles away. They radioed it in to Refugee Rescue, an organization that tries to save refugees from their treacherous sea journeys. Members of Refugee Rescue located the vessel and assessed its integrity. Often the boats carrying refugees across the sea are partially deflated and taking on water. When Refugee Rescue workers arrived, they found a group of twenty-five Afghan refugees, fifteen of them babies and minors. The refugees on the boat had lived in the same village in Afghanistan and had been traveling together to find safety for over six months. Refugee Rescue worked with the Hellenic Coast Guard to bring them to a port. Refugee Rescue reports, "They had tried to cross the Aegean [Sea] ten times, without success. Only after the eleventh attempt did they manage to cross into Greek waters and step onto European soil."[13]

On this occasion, Refugee Rescue workers were able to celebrate their success in saving a group of refugees. Not everyone attempting to cross the sea makes it safely. The group often receives calls for body retrievals. The UNHCR estimates that in 2018, 2,275 people died trying to cross the Mediterranean Sea. In September 2018 alone, twenty-one bodies thought to be migrants washed up on the shores of Spain. Many refugees who tried to cross the sea have never been found.

Dangers on Land and at Sea

While ocean waves are enough to sink a small boat, there are other dangers at sea. Alarm Phone, an emergency hotline for refugees traveling in boats who are in distress, has reported an increased number of attacks on refugee boats in Greek territorial waters. Doaa Al Zamel, a nineteen-year-old Syrian refugee, was on one of these boats. The attackers threw planks of wood at the refugees on board before they rammed their larger boat into the side of the refugee vessel. Al Zamel recalls them yelling, "You dogs! You should've stayed to die in your own country."[14] The boat capsized, and some of the refugees were pulled toward the propeller. Melissa Fleming, a refugee advocate who describes Doaa Al Zamel's journey in detail, explains that Al Zamel "noticed that the sea around her was colored red and realized that people were being sucked into the boat's propeller and dismembered by its blades. Body parts floated all around her. It was worse than anything she'd ever seen during the war in Daraa."[15] Some of the passengers did not know how to swim and drowned immediately. At some point during her four days stranded at sea, Al Zamel witnessed her fiancé die, likely from dehydration and exhaustion. In their dying moments, two strangers handed babies to Al Zamel, who was floating on a small plastic tube. Almost all of the five hundred passengers aboard Al Zamel's boat died before a Japanese tanker rescued her and the two babies she held.

Dangerous sea crossings are not the only hazard endured by refugees. A UNHCR report on refugees' journeys explains, "For many people, the sea crossing is just the final step in a journey that has involved travel through conflict zones or deserts, the danger of kidnapping and torture for ransom, and the threat from traffickers in human beings."[16] This was the experience of seventeen-year-old Sabreen, who fled Yemen during its

> "For many people, the sea crossing is just the final step in a journey that has involved travel through conflict zones or deserts, the danger of kidnapping and torture for ransom, and the threat from traffickers in human beings."[16]
>
> —The United Nations High Commissioner for Refugees

Desperate refugees may undertake dangerous sea voyages in an attempt to reach safety away from their home country. The United Nations High Commission on Refugees estimates that in 2018, 2,275 people died trying to cross the Mediterranean Sea.

civil war (which began in 2015). The UN reports that from March 2015 to March 2019, at least 7,025 civilians were killed and 11,140 injured in the fighting in Yemen.

Sabreen and many others have fled Yemen to find safety. She paid human smugglers $2,200, money from her family, to take her to the coast of Egypt and then across the ocean to Italy. The smugglers tell refugees that they will be traveling in luxury, staying in hotels and on cruise ships with three meals a day and their own room. Sabreen learned this was not the case after having stayed the night in an empty warehouse with concrete floors and no furniture and then boarding a crowded bus with black plastic covering the windows. In her book detailing refugees' harrowing accounts, Malala Yousafzai writes that when some of the passengers on Sabreen's bus complained that they needed water and restrooms, the driver slammed on the brakes, ran up and down the aisle hitting people with his fists, and screamed, "This is not fancy travel! You're refugees. Shut up and stay silent!"[17] When the bus arrived at the coast, the driver threw a woman off the bus and shouted for everyone else to run as fast they could toward the fishing boat that waited for them.

> "This is not fancy travel! You're refugees. Shut up and stay silent!"[17]
>
> —A smuggler on a bus in Egypt

Peril at Day and Night

Before reaching an ocean or an international border, sometimes refugees searching for safety must first make their way through conflict zones so dangerous they can only travel at night. Ajida and her family are Rohingya Muslims, a minority community in Myanmar (formerly known as Burma). The country's 1974 constitution does not recognize them as citizens, making the Rohingya a stateless people. They face discrimination and persecution. Minority Rights Group International explains that the Rohingya "have been particularly targeted for atrocities committed by the Burmese army (the Tatmadaw) such as torture, cruel, inhuman and degrading treatment and punishment, extra-judicial killing and summary execution, arbitrary arrest and detention, rape, destruction of homes, forced labor, forced relocation and eviction, and confiscation of land and property."[18]

Ajida, her husband, and their three young children, ages seven, five and two, woke in the middle of the night to the sound of guns. The Tatmadaw was attacking their village, setting fire to houses, killing the men, and raping the women and girls as part of a systematic genocide that began in October 2016. Ajida's family managed to escape and ran to the forest without any of their belongings. The Tatmadaw were still in the area, so Ajida and her family could not return to their house. They walked only at night all the way to Bangladesh, about 350 miles (563 km). Ajida says,

"Along the way, we passed many bodies—Rohingya who had been shot or hacked to death by the extremist Buddhists who wanted us out. . . . Death was everywhere. We had no choice but to keep moving, or else we might be next."[19]

Refugees' journeys are too often fraught with risks they had not even considered. Many of them suffocate in cargo compartments of trucks used by smugglers. Others die crossing harsh terrain. The UN reports that in 2017, over four hundred people died crossing the desert region along the US-Mexico border. Other refugees have fallen prey to gangs and militias that patrol frequently used routes. Criminal elements are finding that the plight of desperate refugees is lucrative for them. One of the most dangerous countries for refugees in recent years is Libya. An Eritrean woman describes her experience when she traveled for seven days by truck with two other women from Sudan: "[The smugglers] raped us each and every day. At the end of the seven days, the smugglers gave us to the other smugglers in Libya. They kept us locked up for two weeks. They beat us every day. . . . We were supposed to move onwards from that place, but someone kidnapped us. Between us, we had to pay him $6,500 and then he just gave us back to the other smugglers."[20]

Refugees who pay the ransom are often detained again and held for further ransom. Some refugees interviewed for the UNHCR's Telling the Real Story information campaign reported that they were aware of the dangers of traveling through Libya but that it provides the most feasible route to get to Europe across the Mediterranean Sea.

> "Along the way, we passed many bodies—Rohingya who had been shot or hacked to death by the extremist Buddhists who wanted us out. . . . Death was everywhere. We had no choice but to keep moving, or else we might be next."[19]
>
> —Ajida, a Rohingya refugee from Myanmar

Life in Refugee Camps

The conditions in refugee camps vary greatly. Not all refugee camps are as dangerous as those in Libya, but many of them have security problems. Sandra Uwiringiyimana was ten years old when she and her family left the Democratic Republic of the Congo and reached a UN tent camp on the outskirts of neighboring Burundi. At the camp the family had access to food, water, and basic shelter, although they sometimes had to stand in line all day for water. They also received cards for basic food rations like rice, beans, vegetable oil, sugar, salt, flour, soybeans, and corn. Obtaining these supplies, Uwiringiyimana writes, was an uncomfortable experience. "It was as if we had been reduced to beggars."

Ameena Crosses the English Channel

Many teenage refugees make incredibly dangerous journeys on their own to find safety. In the early hours of December 25, 2018, Ameena, a seventeen-year-old Afghan refugee, crossed the English Channel on a 12-foot (3.7 m) dinghy with seven people she did not know. Crossing the world's busiest shipping lane happened only after a journey that took her from Afghanistan through countries that included Iran, Turkey, Greece, and France. Ameena's mother, still at a migration detention center in Athens, Greece, paid the smugglers to get her daughter to England.

Ameena had lived on her own in modest accommodations in France for three months until she was informed that it was her time to make the three-hour trek across the channel. Fortunately, the wind was not too strong, and boat traffic was light because of the Christmas holiday. Even still, when Ameena arrived on England's shore, in the dark at 2:40 a.m., she was vomiting from motion sickness. In an interview with the *Guardian*, Ameena says, "Crossing to the UK was very, very dangerous. . . . It was dark and cold and we were alone, I was scared." She called the police to alert them of her arrival on British soil so that she could apply for asylum, but she did not know her location so they had to find her.

Ultimately, they did find her. She has since been living with a foster family in southwest England. She hopes to attend college and become an airline pilot.

Quoted in Mark Townsend, "Cold, Alone, and Scared: Teenage Refugee Tells of Channel Crossing," *The Guardian* (Manchester), June 9, 2019. www.theguardian.com.

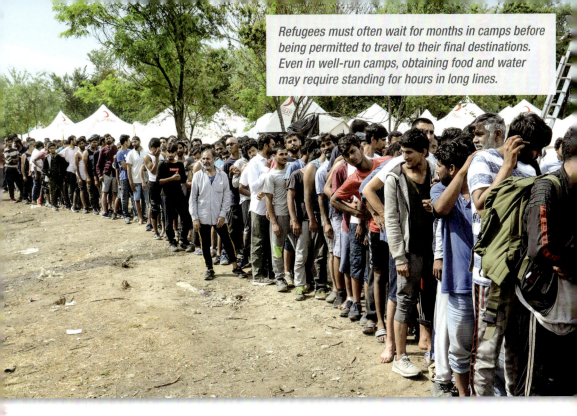

Refugees must often wait for months in camps before being permitted to travel to their final destinations. Even in well-run camps, obtaining food and water may require standing for hours in long lines.

Mom and Dad waited in line with their card for their designated food supply, and it was disheartening to see my parents so powerless."[21] The refugees at Uwiringiyimana's camp were especially powerless when men from Burundi who did not want them there attacked their camp, shooting the refugees and lighting their tents on fire. Sandra's six-year-old sister, Deborah, did not survive the attack, but Sandra and the rest of her family eventually settled in Rochester, New York.

Most refugee camps, like the one Uwiringiyimana's family stayed in, are meant to be temporary. Some however, become permanent settlements. For example, the Palestinian camp of Bourj Al Shamali in southern Lebanon was originally built as a temporary settlement in 1955. Now Bourj Al Shamali is home to third- and fourth-generation refugees. It is near the southern Lebanese city of Tyre and hosts twenty-three thousand registered refugees.

The camp resembles a city in some ways but not in others. There are stone houses and buildings up to eight stories high,

Public Health Problems at a Camp in South Sudan

From late 2013 until September 2018, an estimated 383,000 people were killed in South Sudan's civil war. Two million South Sudanese refugees have fled across international borders in search of safety, but another 2 million people uprooted from their homes still live in the country. Among them, 112,000 people are living in a camp for internally displaced persons in Bentiu, South Sudan. The camp is less than half a square mile (1 sq. km), surrounded with razor wire, and guarded by UN peacekeepers. People arrive there in hopes of finding safety, food, medical assistance, and lost family members. Teresa, a mother of three living in the Bentiu camp, told Doctors Without Borders, "When my village was attacked, many people were separated, and children even ran with different families wherever they were. Everyone was scattered or killed. When we got here, we were only hearing things like, 'This one was killed, this one is here, or this one is looking for you.'"

People living in the Bentiu camp trade their immediate safety concerns for other problems, including the public health issues that come with living in a heavily overcrowded place. For example, latrines overflow, and a thick sludge that flows down a bank brings curious young children to investigate. Over half of the patients requiring medical attention are children under age five. Doctors Without Borders reports, "Many of these children suffer from illnesses like severe acute diarrhea, skin diseases, eye infections, and worms, which can be avoided by improved water and sanitation."

Doctors Without Borders, "South Sudan: Thousands of People Trapped in Poor Conditions at Protection of Civilians Sites," June 20, 2019. www.doctorswithoutborders.org.

---

but the streets and alleys of the camp are not labeled. The unemployment rate in the camp is high, about 60 percent, partly because Lebanon restricts what type of employment Palestinian refugees can have. They cannot work as doctors, engineers, or architects. The people who find work usually spend their days as agricultural laborers working in fields outside the camp. On average, they earn ten dollars per day. There are many children in the camp as well. Claudia Martinez Mansell, a UN humanitarian worker and independent researcher, writes, "More than half the population is under eighteen, and when school gets out they play in the alleys, making up games with sticks, plastic wheels, and whatever else they can find."[22] Despite its similarities to a city and the length of time it has been around, Bourj Al Shamali exists only as a gray blob on the map of Lebanon. A pass is required to enter the camp, which the Lebanese Army guards and monitors.

Women in Danger

The host country is responsible for security in a refugee camp. It is generally provided by the military or local police. Even with security, refugee camps can be dangerous without certain safeguards on the inside. Unaccompanied women and girls are at high risk for sexual exploitation on their journey to safety as well as inside refugee camps.

Bathroom facilities in refugee camps are a particularly dangerous point for women and girls. The facilities are supposed to be separated by gender and have locks on the doors, but that is

Women refugees face challenges that men usually do not. They may fall victim to sexual assault or be forced into marriage or prostitution.

not always the case. Even when the bathrooms are separated, many women have reported fear of using them at night because of the poor lighting. Adèle, a Syrian refugee living in a camp in Greece, says, "[The] shower in the camp is cold and there is no lock. Men walk in when you are inside. There are no lights in the toilets. At night, sometimes I go to the toilet with my sister or pee in a bucket."[23]

There are some refugee camps that have become bases for organized prostitution rings and sex trafficking. The Cara di Mineo camp on the Italian island of Sicily is one of the largest camps in Europe. In 2018 it housed about four thousand people, many of whom were asylum seekers and migrants from Africa. Barbie Latza Nadeau, a reporter for the *Guardian*, writes, "Cara di Mineo . . . has become a hunting ground for traffickers. Posing as asylum seekers, traffickers lure women out of the centre on the pretext of shopping trips or other excursions, and deliver them to the Nigerian women who control forced prostitution rings. They are then forced into sex work under the threat of violence."[24] According to the International Organization for Migration, over 80 percent of the women brought from Nigeria to Europe are unknowingly on trips paid for by sex traffickers. The migrants generally believe they are going to work at a hair salon or somewhere similar. The traffickers trap them into these rings, such as the one near Cara di Mineo, where they are forced to work off their debts by prostituting themselves.

Refugees fleeing war and persecution often face additional dangers as they attempt to make their way to safety. Yet the hazards of remaining in a deeply troubled homeland are in many cases simply too great. That the numbers of refugees continues to swell reflects their desperation for what everyone wants—peace and stability.

CHAPTER THREE

Hurdles and Outcomes for Refugee Status

Rahaf Mohammed, an eighteen-year-old refugee from Saudi Arabia, had a difficult time convincing authorities that she met the criteria for refugee status. She had asserted her independence and renounced Islam, a crime punishable by death in Saudi Arabia. She said she wanted to be able to marry the person she chose, travel freely, and get a job without someone's permission, none of which were possibilities for her if she lived with her family in Saudi Arabia. Mohammed referred to herself as a prisoner of her family and described years of alleged abuse. For example, she said that she was locked up for six months for cutting her own hair.

On January 5, 2019, while she and her family were visiting Kuwait, Mohammed fled. Over the next several days, she made her way to Thailand, where she was apprehended by Saudi officials. They took her passport and threatened to send her back home. She feared that she would be killed if she were sent back to her family in Saudi Arabia, so she barricaded herself in an airport hotel room, asked for asylum, and appealed to the public on Twitter for help. She also wrote a suicide note while trapped in Thailand. In an interview, Mohammed said, "During this time, I was thinking about what kind of goodbye messages I

"During this time, I was thinking about what kind of goodbye messages I would write, because I was not going to allow them to take me. I was prepared to end my life before they kidnapped me."[25]

—Rahaf Mohammed, an eighteen-year-old Saudi refugee facing threat of deportation

Rahaf Mohammed's (center) quest for refugee status to escape her family's abuse drew international attention in 2019. Eventually Canada accepted her as a refugee.

would write, because I was not going to allow them to take me. I was prepared to end my life before they kidnapped me."[25]

Mohammed's case attracted worldwide attention. Human Rights Watch and several journalists advocated for her while she was in Thailand. The UN assessed her claim for refugee status, and Canada accepted her as a refugee. In a media statement, Mohammed acknowledged that she was "one of the lucky ones."[26] Many women who experience persecution by their families never gain the attention that Mohammed did. Those who manage to escape are often caught and deported. Some face death when they return.

Gender Hurdles for Refugee Status

The legal definition of *refugee* was devised in Europe following World War II, and many argue that it is out of date. It focuses on acts of persecution that are committed by state actors, like Germany's Nazi Party. The problem today is that millions, like Mohammed, face persecution committed by non-state actors, such as family. Kennji Kizuka, an asylum attorney and senior researcher at Human Rights First, explains, "Many judges [hearing asylum cases] don't see the violence by these non-state actors as rising to the level of political opinion. [They] don't see the violence as having any political dimension."[27] In short, gendered violence, like assault and rape, is often not grounds for asylum unless the perpetrators are state actors, such as soldiers, and the persecution is committed systematically against women of a particular ethnic group, such as the Rohingya in Myanmar.

Also, a refugee must be outside of his or her country of origin for consideration. Aside from financial constraints to traveling outside of one's country, women in countries like Saudi Arabia have more difficulties traveling because of their gender. When Mohammed fled, she had to wait until she was with her family in Kuwait. It was not until August 2019 that Saudi women above age twenty-one could travel independently without permission from a male family member. Women and girls also face more dangerous journeys from their home countries due to increased risk of sexual violence and assault, child marriage, and exploitation. They account for almost three-quarters of human trafficking victims. In short, women refugees sometimes face overwhelming challenges in leaving their countries of origin.

There are many women like Mohammed who are fleeing domestic violence. The UN agency UN Women estimates that 35 percent of women worldwide have experienced abuse from a partner during their lifetime, with some national studies showing up to 70 percent of women have experienced abuse. UN Women also estimates that eighty-seven thousand women were intentionally killed globally in 2017, over half of them by an intimate partner. When women flee these situations, the burden of proof is problematic for them. Their testimonies become the centerpieces of their cases. Some of the refugees come from cultures in which it is shameful to discuss matters of sexual violence, particularly when the interpreters, judges, and advocates are men. Sandra Uwiringiyimana was sexually assaulted by her cousin's husband in East Africa when she was eleven years old after the attack on her refugee camp in Burundi. She explains that there is a culture of silence around sexual assault and that if a woman talks, she might be shunned by her family. She writes, "In many cultures, including mine, young women who are sexually abused are often blamed and rejected by their communities. . . . There wasn't even really a word for 'rape' in my native language. But I kept it to myself. I locked it away."[28]

In some countries, decision makers view domestic violence as a private matter and not as one of the categories of persecution (race, religion, nationality, membership in a particular social group, and political opinion). In June 2018 US attorney general Jeff Sessions said that victims of domestic abuse and gang violence do not qualify for asylum. Sessions argued that his decision helps reduce immigration backlogs and "restores sound principles of asylum and long-standing principles of immigration law."[29] The question of whether gendered violence provides grounds for asylum is determined by each country primarily on the basis of whether "gender" is interpreted as being part of the "membership of a particular social group" category in the definition of *refugee*. In the case of Mohammed, renouncing Islam when she arrived in Thailand put her in imminent danger on religious grounds, not just because she was a woman fleeing from her family.

The Waiting Game
In addition to gender, there are many other barriers to acquiring refugee status. Financial resources, language, the danger associated with crossing an international border, and access to information are all hurdles. But the most significant among them is

The Refugee Olympic Team

When Jamal Abdelmaji Eisa Mohammed fled Sudan at age seventeen and spent three days crossing the Sinai desert from Egypt to Israel, he likely did not imagine that eight years later, in 2019, he would be competing in an international athletic competition. Mohammed was granted asylum in Israel, where he earned enough money painting houses to support his mother, sister, and two brothers, who were staying at a refugee camp in Sudan after his father was killed in an attack on their village. In Tel Aviv, Israel, Mohammed joined a running club whose members included refugees and other young athletes from disadvantaged neighborhoods. In 2017 he received an Olympic scholarship that enabled him to train full time. Mohammed was hoping to compete in the 5,000-meter race in Tokyo's Olympic Games in 2020.

He would not be the first refugee to do so. For the first time ever, a team of refugee athletes competed at the 2016 Summer Games in Rio de Janeiro, Brazil. Two Syrian swimmers, two judokas from the Democratic Republic of the Congo, a marathon runner from Ethiopia, and five middle-distance runners from South Sudan came together to form the Refugee Olympic Team. Thomas Bach, president of the International Olympic Committee, says, "The Refugee Olympic athletes were some of the stars of these Olympic Games. . . . They demonstrated what you can achieve if you want to. They also demonstrated that they are not simply refugees, but that they are human beings."

Quoted in UNHCR, "International Olympic Committee." www.unhcr.org.

arguably time. It takes the United States an average of two years to navigate through the security and administrative procedures of a refugee case for the people who are selected, which constitutes only a very small percentage of the people eligible for resettlement. Others wait for much longer. Many refugees choose to return to unsafe conditions in their own countries rather than spend a lifetime in limbo at a refugee camp.

Mahmoud Abdelwahab, twenty-five years old, left his job as a cook and fled war-torn Mosul, Iraq, in 2016. He embarked on a journey during which he witnessed a boat capsize and multiple people die. He eventually arrived in Vienna, Austria, where he applied for asylum. There he waited among Europe's 158,000 refugees hoping to be resettled. He was not permitted to work and did not have the opportunity to learn German. All he could do was wait. Two years after his arrival in the country, his path to resettlement did not seem any more likely than when he arrived. He made the tough decision to return home. In the spring of 2018, Austria offered 1,000 euros and a one-way flight to refugees who would leave on their own. Abdelwahab took the money with the intent to buy a car and become a cab driver in Iraq. During an interview with NPR before his departure, he reflected on the time he spent in Europe hoping to be granted refugee status. "Two years . . . [I] was here for nothing. It didn't make any sense to come here."[30] NPR reached out to him after the interview but has not heard from him since he returned to Iraq.

Refugees who manage to make it to a refugee camp may find themselves waiting for years to have their case processed. In some instances, refugees choose to return home to the dangerous conditions in their native countries rather than remain in limbo indefinitely.

Applying for Refugee Status

Each country has its own process to determine whether a person is eligible for refugee status. Some nations have a more strict interpretation and grant fewer cases than others. This process, called Refugee Status Determination (RSD), is primarily the responsibility of individual host countries, but the UNHCR handles refugee requests for countries that do not have a system in place. In 2017 the UNHCR registered over 250,000 new refugee applications, making it the second-largest RSD institution in the world. While the UNHCR has the ability to determine refugee status, it does not have the ability to provide asylum for a refugee. In Mohammed's case, for example, the UNHCR determined that she was eligible for refugee status, but Canada provided asylum.

Nations that are members of the 1951 Refugee Convention and/or the 1967 protocol incorporate the guiding agreement into their own domestic laws. Those laws typically reflect the priorities of the specific country. For example, US Citizenship and Immigration Services states that a refugee is someone who "Is located outside of the United States; Is of special humanitarian concern to the United States; Demonstrates that they were persecuted or fear persecution due to race, religion, nationality, political opinion, or membership in a particular social group; Is not firmly resettled in another country; Is admissible to the United States."[31]

In the United States, refugees must receive a referral from a UNHCR field office to the United States Refugee Admissions Program. Applicants begin with a series of interviews and other checks aimed at verifying their identity. These checks seek to eliminate anyone who has connections to terrorist groups, a criminal history, past immigration violations, or a communicable disease such as tuberculosis, HIV/AIDS, or hepatitis.

Telling Their Stories

Immigration officials have only a short time to ask questions and collect information in the determination interview, usually about an hour. Therefore, it is important for applicants to understand the criteria used to evaluate their claims. Not all traumatic incidents are relevant. For example, some people might witness a horrific event in which several people are brutally killed, but the incident is not relevant to the interview unless the applicant is more likely to be a victim of such an attack because of his or her ethnicity or religion. Also, lawyers and advocates encourage refugees to provide more details that will help the interviewers fairly assess their cases. Instead of stating that the police in their country cannot be trusted, refugee advocate Katy Murdza explains "that applicants should provide examples of when they or people they know asked the authorities for help, and received none."[32]

Refugees who get support in the application process from translators and lawyers significantly improve their chance for a successful application. Dina Nayeri, author of *The Ungrateful Refugee: What Immigrants Never Tell You*, describes an Iranian volunteer at a refugee camp in the Netherlands named Ahmed Pouri, who helps refugees frame their stories. She writes:

> "To be seen, refugees must learn to tell their stories the Dutch way, or the British way, or the American way."[33]
>
> —Dina Nayeri, author of *The Ungrateful Refugee: What Immigrants Never Tell You*

> I call him The Refugee Whisperer. People passed his phone number around at camps, in prisons, in homes of settled countrymen. From lawyer to client, refugee to refugee, everyone knew his name. And his job? To help asylum seekers translate *themselves*, their culture, the tangible life they left behind. . . . To be seen, refugees must learn to tell their stories the Dutch way, or the British way, or the American way.[33]

But even when refugees have a compelling story and meet all of the criteria, sometimes there are other factors that prevent them from resettling in certain countries.

Vetoing Refugees

Muna Muday fled from the civil war in Somalia with her family when she was a child. They had been cleared to settle in the United States and were waiting at a camp in Kenya for their travel documents, but then the terrorist attacks of September 11, 2001, happened. At that time, US policy makers suspended all pending refugee resettlements, and Muday and her family had to remain in the Kenyan refugee camp until 2004, at which point they resettled in Nashville, Tennessee.

Muday now attends Vanderbilt University, where she is working on a master's degree in public health. But memories of the extra years her family spent in a refugee camp have resurfaced. In September 2019 President Donald Trump issued an executive order allowing states and cities to veto refugee resettlements. She fears that refugees will suffer under this policy. In an interview with NPR, Muday said, "It's very sad to see that . . . a leader of our nation [would] do this to people that really need the help."

In October 2019 there were zero refugees resettled in the United States. According to World Relief, a refugee resettlement agency, this had not happened in the thirty years since the 1980 Refugee Act. Refugee advocates fear that allowing states and cities to veto refugee settlements will further decimate the United States' resettlement program.

Quoted in Joel Rose, "What Happens When States Have the Power to Reject Refugees," *All Things Considered*, NPR, November 11, 2019. www.npr.org.

Numbers

Each country determines how many refugees it is willing to accept. More often than not, there are more people seeking refugee resettlement than the number of available spaces. Historically, the United States has been among the top countries in the world for refugee resettlement. However, the Trump administration lowered the refugee ceiling from 110,000 refugees in 2017 to 45,000 in 2018, to 30,000 in 2019, and down to 18,000 in 2020. In the past few years the majority of US refugee admissions have been from Africa and eastern Asia. In 2018 the top countries of origin for US refugees were the Democratic Republic of the Congo, Myanmar, Ukraine, and Bhutan.

When applicants are denied refugee status in the United States, they remain where they are, most likely in a refugee camp. By definition, they are not in the United States when they apply, so deportation is not relevant. This is much different from the immigration process for asylum seekers, who apply on US soil and are held in detention centers. Unlike refugees, asylum seekers are deported to their country of origin if their case for asylum is rejected. The next steps for refugees if their application is declined might include remaining in the refugee settlement, returning to their home country, or applying to another country as a refugee. While there is not a US appeals process, if the US Department of Homeland Security denies a person refugee status, the applicant may request a reconsideration of his or her case based on new information. The decision to reconsider is up to the department.

Resettlement

On average, successful refugee applicants wait eighteen to twenty-four months to be resettled in the United States. The International Organization for Migration makes the travel arrangements to the United States. Once refugees arrive, local agencies help them find housing and jobs. These agencies also help with school enrollment and other logistics of resettlement. Often refugee families are assigned a volunteer who can guide them and answer questions about everything from shopping in supermarkets to using public transportation.

There are about 190 refugee resettlement communities across the United States. In 2019 Texas settled the largest number of newly arrived refugees, about 9 percent of the total. Other large refugee resettlement states in 2019 included Washington, California, and New York. Refugees of particular nationalities are more likely to settle in certain states. For example, Iraqis account for the largest refugee population in Michigan, Nebraska, and Massachusetts, while the biggest group of refugees in Delaware and Montana came from Eritrea. Minnesota has the largest concentration of Somalis in the United States, with fifty-two thousand people reporting Somali ancestry to the US Census Bureau in

2017, and 80 percent of them living in Minneapolis. Refugees who come to the United States frequently discuss the conditions of the city in which they resettle with their friends and family members. Abdisalam Adam, a Somali American, told the Minnesota Historical Society, "When the people in the refugee camps heard about the early arrivals that came here and were well received, they reported back to their relatives."[34]

Preparation for resettlement begins even before refugees leave for their newly adopted country. But often that preparation is minimal. Before their departure from the refugee camp in Burundi, for instance, Uwiringiyimana and her family received cultural counseling through a translator. Uwiringiyimana says, "I remember the translator giving us this

In the United States, local agencies help refugees with jobs, housing, school enrollment, and other challenges related to settling in a new country. Here, teacher Tanner Faris of Boise, Idaho, helps Ruth Gakuru and Rina Urayeneza understand grocery pricing.

piece of advice as well: 'When you get to America, don't stare at people. Don't point.' I thought that was funny. As if we would go around staring and pointing at people!"[35]

There was a lot more to learn once Uwiringiyimana and her family reached New York City, where she was initially shocked by the pervasive use of cell phones. The temperature was also much colder than her family had expected or ever experienced. When they first arrived in the city, there was a snowstorm. In an interview, she recalls, "It was so scary. I thought, oh my goodness, these people live in ice."[36] When they arrived at their new house in Rochester, New York, they were pleased to find that the kitchen was already stocked with food, but the food in the United States was very different. Uwiringiyimana thought she was looking at a package of pink worms in the refrigerator, only to later learn that it was ground beef. She learned English by watching cartoons and taking formal classes.

A Long Wait

Getting refugee status is usually a long and tedious process. Wait times for refugees are prolonged. Procedural hurdles, national debates over resettlements, and ongoing wars continue to swell resident numbers in already overcrowded refugee camps around the world. Meanwhile refugees wait for solutions and a place to call home. While in limbo, many of them try to live their lives and maintain a normal schedule. In the camps, they participate in traditional dances, make noodles, play soccer, and revel in the small joys that remind them of a happier place.

> "I remember the translator giving us this piece of advice as well: 'When you get to America, don't stare at people. Don't point.' I thought that was funny. As if we would go around staring and pointing at people!"[35]
>
> —Sandra Uwiringiyimana, a refugee from the Democratic Republic of the Congo

CHAPTER FOUR

The US Response

Refugee policy in the United States is fraught with disagreement. While one side of the debate argues that the United States should take in more refugees to help alleviate the global crisis, others believe the costs and risks of refugee resettlement are too great to do so. The Trump administration espouses the latter view. In addition to reducing the refugee ceiling, Trump has instituted a policy that makes it more difficult for refugees—especially those from Muslim-majority countries, including Somalia, Iran, Syria, and Yemen—to gain refugee status in the United States.

The political debate has gained so much momentum that President Donald Trump spoke about it at an October 2019 campaign rally in Minneapolis, Minnesota—a city that has openly welcomed refugees from Somalia and other countries. He said:

> For many years, leaders in Washington brought large numbers of refugees to your state from Somalia without considering the impact on schools and communities and taxpayers. I promised you that as president I would give local communities a greater say in refugee policy and put in place enhanced vetting and responsible immigration control. . . . We are keeping terrorists, criminals, and extremists the hell out of our country.[37]

Prior to the Trump administration's multiyear reductions to the refugee ceiling, the United States had been the world leader in refugee resettlement since World War II. That is no longer the case. The per capita refugee resettlement rates are now higher in Canada, Australia, Sweden, and Norway than in the United States. In September 2019 the Trump administration proposed a deeper cut to refugee admissions, down to 18,000 for 2020, the lowest ceiling in the thirty-year history of the refugee program detailed in the Refugee Act of 1980. Critics of the administration's refugee policy argue that countries worldwide, with the United States foremost among them, have abandoned their humanitarian responsibilities. Nazanin Ash, an International Rescue Committee official, argues, "What we see now is a global race to the bottom in meeting humanitarian obligations. And it's led by the U.S."[38] Debates surrounding the issue of refugee resettlement are occurring in host countries around the world.

> "What we see now is a global race to the bottom in meeting humanitarian obligations. And it's led by the U.S."[38]
>
> —Nazanin Ash, International Rescue Committee official

Refugees as a Threat to National Security?

US presidents have traditionally honored the agreements of their predecessors, even if they did not agree with them. Former president Barack Obama made a deal at the end of his term in 2016 with Australian prime minister Malcolm Turnbull to accept 1,250 to 2,000 refugees who were being held in Australian detention centers on remote islands in the South Pacific. In a phone call on January 28, 2017, Trump told Turnbull he thought the arrangement was "disgusting." He had concerns about the refugees and argued, "I guarantee you they are bad. That is why they are in prison." During the conversation, Trump mentioned three notorious attacks when he added, "Does anybody know who these people are? Are they going to become the Boston bomber in five years? I do not want to have more San Bernardinos or World Trade Centers."[39]

Ali Reza Ataie and Ali Hesar were among the vetted and cleared refugees from the Australian detention center. The two boys are from persecuted minorities in Afghanistan. Their families sent them away when they were fifteen years old, hoping that they would find a better and safer life in Australia. Their journeys took them through India, Malaysia, and Indonesia, where they boarded a dangerously overcrowded fishing boat that was headed for Australia. What they did not know is that Australia had passed a policy in 2013 banning asylum to people arriving in boats. Australian government officials claim the ban is meant to deter human smuggling, but some human rights organizations suggest it is motivated by xenophobia, a fear of people from other countries. Because of the ban, Ataie and Hesar were intercepted and brought to a detention center in Nauru, a small island nation near Australia. They were held there for three years. Detainees in Nauru stayed in tents, were allowed only two-minute showers, and were called by their numbers rather than their names. Ataie says, "We had gone through all of these countries, gone through the ocean. And then we were in prison. It was the most terrible situation of my life."[40]

Donald Trump addresses a crowd in November 2019. The Trump Administration has tightened immigration policies, lengthening the asylum application process and making it more cumbersome.

Because of the agreement between Obama and Turnbull, which Trump eventually honored, Ataie and Hesar, now twenty-two years old, are living near Dallas, Texas. They work full time and volunteer in the refugee community, and Ataie studies cybersecurity online. They, among others from the Australian detention center, cleared rigorous background checks and are not the criminals Trump described. The transcript from the conversation between Trump and Turnbull that subsequently was leaked to the press, however, shows the national security concerns that sometimes arise in connection with refugee policy.

Refugees and Terrorism

There is a connection between some refugee arrivals in Germany with terrorist plots in Europe from 2014 to 2017. In December 2016 a rejected Tunisian asylum seeker hijacked a large truck and drove it into the crowded Christmas market in Berlin, killing twelve people and injuring fifty-six others. Over a two-week period in the summer of 2016, there was a series of smaller attacks by asylum seekers. These attacks included a seventeen-year-old Afghan asylum seeker's ax rampage on a German commuter train and a Syrian refugee's attempted suicide bombing of an outdoor concert, which left only the perpetrator dead. Many policy makers around the world cite these attacks as support for the view that refugees are linked to terrorism. For example, during the phone call with Turnbull in January 2017, Trump said, "Look at what has happened in Germany. Look at what is happening in these countries. These people are crazy to let this happen. . . . Germany is a mess because of what happened."[41]

In 2019 the Cato Institute (a libertarian Washington, DC, think tank) published a risk assessment study of terrorist attacks in the United States. It found that terrorists are much more likely to be travelers with tourist visas than they are to be refugees. Since 1975, of the 192 attacks on US soil perpetrated by foreign-born terrorists, 25 were carried out by refugees. During the same time period, the United States had accepted more than 3 million refugees.

In December 2016 a rejected Tunisian asylum seeker drove a large truck into the crowded Christmas market in Berlin, Germany, killing twelve people and injuring fifty-six others. Immigration critics said the incident proved their claim that many refugees are linked to terrorism.

The majority of foreign-born terrorist attacks (65 percent) on US soil involved Islamists. The higher percentage of Islamist attacks has affected refugee policy in the United States. Trump's travel ban, the executive order temporarily barring refugees from Muslim-majority countries, significantly reduced the flow of refugees coming from Syria and other countries. Americans are evenly divided in their opinions on resettling Syrian refugees in the United States. A 2018 Pew Research Center poll asked whether the United States has a responsibility to accept refugees from Syria; 48 percent of respondents replied no, 47 percent said yes, and the remaining 5 percent were uncertain.

VIEWPOINT

The United States Should Lower Its Refugee Ceiling

Kevin McAleenan, secretary of the US Department of Homeland Security, supports lowering the US refugee ceiling. With thousands of asylum seekers waiting for processing at the US-Mexico border, he believes government resources should be focused on these individuals rather than on refugees abroad.

> The Administration's proposal for refugee admissions in Fiscal Year 2020 will allow the Department of Homeland Security to focus on addressing the ongoing crisis at the southern border, reducing a staggering asylum backlog that unfairly delays relief for those with meritorious claims, and completing more overall cases in an increasingly multifaceted humanitarian workload.

Quoted in Priscilla Alvarez, "US Sets a Refugee Cap of 18,000 for Next Year—a New Historic Low," CNN, September 26, 2019. www.cnn.com.

Many critics of the Trump administration's travel ban argue that the ban does not address the terrorists entering as tourists, or terrorists who are already American citizens. Matthew Levitt, director of the Stein Program on Counterterrorism & Intelligence at the Washington Institute for Near East Foreign Policy, explains, "Today's most immediate threats are mostly from homegrown violent extremists who act in small groups or as lone offenders. Stopping people from certain countries from entering the United States does not address this problem."[42]

Critics of the travel ban also suggest that Islamophobia, or fear of Muslims, should not be a basis for policy. However, Trump addresses his critics by arguing, "This [travel ban] is not about religion—this is about terror and keeping our country safe."[43] Other supporters of the ban echo the president's sentiment and hail it as a necessary tool for national security. In June 2018 the Supreme Court upheld Trump's travel ban. Chief Justice John Roberts argued that because the countries listed constituted only 8 percent of the world's Muslim population, the ban was not religiously hostile to Muslims and was in the realm of the president's authority.

VIEWPOINT

The United States Should Not Lower Its Refugee Ceiling

Jack Reed, a Democratic senator from Rhode Island, believes that lowering the refugee ceiling will put many people at risk and reduce US global influence. In a letter to President Donald Trump, he and fifteen other US senators urge the president to uphold the tradition of the United States as a safe haven for refugees worldwide.

> We urge you to heed the recommendation of top U.S. military officials and faith leaders to open our doors to eligible refugees from all corners of the world. We know that returning refugees to their countries of origin would put their lives in immediate danger and would perpetuate the very cycle of violence from which they sought to escape. A generous U.S. refugee policy spares tens of thousands from terrible fates.

Quoted in Jack Reed, United States Senator for Rhode Island, "Reed Urges Trump Not to Cut Refugee Admissions to All-Time Low," September 27, 2019. www.reed.senate.gov.

Burden Versus Contribution

One of the reasons the Trump administration cites for lowering the refugee ceiling is that refugee resettlement is costly. Stephen Miller, Trump's senior policy adviser, is considered the architect of much of the administration's immigration policy. In a book by a former White House communications aide, Miller is quoted as saying, "I would be happy if not a single refugee foot ever again touched American soil."[44] According to the *New York Times*, Miller believes that refugees are more likely to be unskilled and uneducated, and therefore "drains on the American economy."[45]

Research from the US Department of Health and Human Services (HHS), however, suggests that refugees have a positive effect on the economy. The HHS report, submitted in July 2017, finds that "refugees brought in $63 million more in government revenues over the past decade than they cost."[46] The White House rejected these findings. Through a spokesperson, it cited a different conclusion, which is that "refugees with few skills coming from war-torn countries take more government benefits from the Department of Health and Human Services than the average population, and are not a new benefit to the U.S. economy."[47]

In the end, the report submitted to the Trump administration included only the costs of HHS programs (such as Medicaid, temporary financial assistance, and food stamps) and excluded the findings of the benefits of refugees. The final report found that refugees, particularly in their first four years in the United States, are more likely than the rest of the population to use the HHS programs.

> "Refugees with few skills coming from war-torn countries take more government benefits from the Department of Health and Human Services than the average population, and are not a new benefit to the U.S. economy."[47]
>
> —White House spokesperson

Asylum Cases Influence Refugee Policy

Concerns about national security and the costs of resettlement have played a significant role in shaping US refugee policy, as has the rising number of asylum seekers already in the United States. The United States has been inundated with asylum seekers who are fleeing violence and gangs in Mexico and the Northern Triangle countries of El Salvador, Guatemala, and Honduras. An unprecedented number of undocumented migrants—nearly 1 million in 2019, according to US Customs and Border Protection—have flooded the southwestern border and strained resources. As US officials address the migration crisis on the border, hospitality to refugees has taken a backseat.

Giron Martinez, a twenty-three-year-old student activist and member of a Honduran opposition party, fled his country in October 2018. He took this step after his friends were murdered and police threatened him with death for his participation in demonstrations for justice and against government corruption. Martinez walked about 2,500 miles (4,023 km) from Honduras to Tijuana, Mexico. He then waited there for two months with other migrants to be granted admission to the San Ysidro Port of Entry near San Diego. He was held there for a week before being transferred to a series of prisonlike detainment facilities in Louisiana and Mississippi, where he spent the next eight months. During the course of his asylum application process, he applied for parole from detention facilities three times. Despite the fact that he had no criminal history, had the support of a US citizen sponsor, was not a flight risk, and had passed his credible fear interview (whereby he was found to have a legitimate concern about undergoing torture or persecution if he returned home), he was still denied parole. After the arduous journey and long detainment process, Martinez was finally granted asylum. He was released in September 2019 and moved to Los Angeles, California.

Women fleeing poverty and violence in their native Honduras climb onto a truck in Oaxaca, Mexico, during their journey to the United States.

There are thousands of other stories like Martinez's in the United States. Asylum seeker numbers are not reflected in the refugee admission statistics. The asylum application process takes anywhere from six months to a few years. In the meantime, applicants like Martinez are held in detention centers, one of the two hundred immigration prisons scattered across the United States, as they wait with others who have cases in the massive backlog.

Asylum seeker and refugee application processes use the same pool of resources. In September 2019 acting director of the USCIS Ken Cuccinelli said that the agency had a backlog of 330,000 asylum cases. In an official statement, the US Department of State cited the backlog as support for Trump's lowered refugee ceiling for 2020. State Department officials argue, "The current burdens on the U.S. immigration system must be alleviated before it is again possible to resettle large number of refugees. Prioritizing the humanitarian protection cases of those already in our country is simply a matter of fairness and common sense."[48]

> "The current burdens on the U.S. immigration system must be alleviated before it is again possible to resettle large number of refugees."[48]
>
> —US Department of State

Global debates over refugee resettlement are occurring at the forefront of US domestic politics. The reduced refugee ceiling is significantly affecting the total resettlement numbers worldwide. Some people who realize they are unlikely to get refugee status in the United States take a different route. They pay smugglers to get them to Mexico so they can make attempts as asylum seekers at the US border. All systems are overloaded, and backlogs will take a long time to clear—far longer than the duration of any one presidential administration.

CHAPTER FIVE

In Search of a Global Solution

Linda, a nineteen-year-old Syrian refugee, hoped to settle in Denmark, where her fiancé already lived. The first challenge was getting there. In May 2018 Linda embarked on a border crossing from Turkey to Greece arranged by human smugglers. She took a minibus with thirty-five other people that drove from Istanbul to the northwestern Turkish city of Edirne. Under the cover of darkness one night, the refugees boarded boats to cross the Evros River. In the month prior, thirty-six hundred refugees had crossed the river; it was the first time since 2012 that more people had arrived via the river than by sea. The people living in the region were surprised by and unprepared for the large number of refugees crossing the Evros. Typically, when the refugees make it to Greek soil, they discard their life jackets on the banks of the river and wait in long lines at police stations to file their asylum applications.

Linda never had the opportunity to apply. When she stepped onto Greek soil, men wearing dark uniforms and carrying guns stopped the group, which included children and pregnant women, and took away their mobile phones. Linda describes her experience: "They beat the men who were with us, put us in a boat, and sent us back to the Turkish side of the border."[49] The group immediately attempted another failed crossing. They made it a little farther into Greece the second time, but the same thing happened, and they were forced on the boat back to Turkey. By the time Turkish soldiers found them, they had not had drinking water in two days, and some of them were sick from drinking contaminated water from the river. The soldiers brought them food, water, and milk and arranged for taxis to drive them to Istanbul. Not everyone has been so fortunate.

Since 2016 there has been an increase in Turkish political dissidents fleeing for Greece. The Turkish government has jailed tens of thousands of these people, including Murat Çapan, who tried to seek asylum in Greece. In May 2017 Murat, a journalist for the magazine *Nokta*, crossed the Evros River and was forced back to Turkey. According to the Hellenic League for Human Rights, he is now serving twenty-two and a half years in prison after having been prosecuted for "participating in a terrorist organization and attempting to overthrow the constitution."[50] In cases like Murat's, pushback leads to the persecution of the would-be asylum seeker. Pushbacks are illegal under both European and international laws on refugee protection, but they are occurring openly. Among other recommendations to help alleviate the global refugee crisis, the UNHCR is calling for an end to pushbacks, which are an obstruction of the asylum application process. Arguing against pushbacks, Leo Dobbs, a UNHCR spokesperson in Greece, says, "The right to claim and enjoy asylum is a fundamental human right."[51]

> "The right to claim and enjoy asylum is a fundamental human right."[51]
>
> —Leo Dobbs, a UNHCR spokesperson in Greece

Safety in Transit

Putting an end to pushbacks is one way to improve refugees' safety in transit, but there are many others as well. International refugee aid agencies have called for stronger prosecution efforts against human traffickers. They argue that traffickers are making substantial profits from the desperation of refugees and that more severe penalties would deter them. Not only are traffickers putting the refugees in unsafe circumstances, like in overloaded small boats navigating the ocean and in trucks crossing the desert, they are sometimes torturing and raping them en route. "This means not only that human trafficking must be a criminal offence in the country where an act of trafficking is detected, but also that the law must be enforced,"[52] explains the United Nations Office on Drugs and Crime (UNODC), which works to increase the global number of human trafficking convictions.

> "Without specialised human trafficking laws, victims are subjected to greater uncertainties while traffickers face reduced risks and penalties."[53]
>
> —The United Nations Office on Drugs and Crime

Many countries do not have legislation that is specific to refugees and economic migrants but instead focuses only on the sexual exploitation of women and children. The UNODC argues, "Without specialised human trafficking laws, victims are subjected to greater uncertainties while traffickers face reduced risks and penalties."[53] Passage of these laws is not enough, however. Border guards, police, prosecutors, judges, and others need to be properly trained in dealing with human traffickers if the laws are to be effective.

Finding and prosecuting human smuggling gangs would likely help to reduce the number of people crossing the sea in unsafe vessels. It would not, however, completely eliminate refugees' perilous sea crossings, thereby justifying the need for search and rescue operations. Crossing the ocean is arguably the most dangerous part of a refugee's journey, and deaths, particularly on the Mediterranean Sea, are on the rise. According to the UNHCR, in 2018 there was one death for every 51 arrivals, up from one death per 269 arrivals in 2015. In September 2018, a particularly deadly month, there was one death at sea for every 8 arrivals.

Nongovernmental organizations (NGOs) that conduct search and rescue operations, such as Doctors Without Borders and Save the Children, have come under intense criticism. Some Europeans refer to these vessels as "migrant taxis" and suggested their presence was helping human smugglers get refugees to European soil. On October 5, 2018, twenty-two people stormed

Demonstrators in France show their support for nongovernmental organizations (NGOs) that conduct search and rescue operations by boat in the Mediterranean Sea. Although intended to rescue refugees in trouble, these operations have received criticism from those who believe they aid human smugglers.

the headquarters of SOS Méditerranée in France in protest of that organization's search and rescue operations. Italy restricted NGOs' search and rescue capabilities in the Mediterranean Sea and impounded some of their boats. Many people advocating for refugees' rights and safety are suggesting that these restrictions should be lifted to prevent more loss of life at sea. Others argue that governments have a moral obligation to conduct search and rescue operations and not rely on NGOs to do it. In either case, in order to reduce refugee casualties at sea, refugee advocates urge governments to increase patrols in the Mediterranean and lift the restrictions on NGOs.

Getting Libya to the Table

Libya, directly south of Italy across the Mediterranean Sea, is a gateway country for millions of African refugees on their way to Europe. At some point in their journey, many of these people end up in migrant camps. Some are run by militias that profit from smuggling and extorting refugees. Other camps are run by groups supported by the European Union and Libyan Coast Guard. The UNHCR estimates that there are five thousand to six thousand people being held in the various camps in Libya. None of these camps truly offer safety to refugees. The living conditions are abhorrent in both kinds of camps. There have been multiple reports of assault and torture at these camps. Deutsche Welle, a German-owned public broadcasting company, reports, "They are overcrowded, people are starving and almost every woman is a victim of sexual attacks."[54] Reports of refugees and migrants being sold as slaves have also surfaced.

Sunday Iabarot, a thirty-two-year-old migrant, left Nigeria in 2016. He planned to cross the Mediterranean Sea from Libya to reach Italy, where he had heard from friends on Facebook that there were many job opportunities. When he crossed the southern border of Libya, he met a taxi driver who offered to drive him to the coast. Instead, the driver sold him to another man for $200. Iabarot's captor told him that he must work on a construction site to pay off his debt. Any time he refused to work, he was beaten and did not get food. When he tried to run away, his captor punished him by carving a giant number *3* on the left side of his face with a fire-heated knife. If the number had significance to the captors, it remains unknown to Iabarot. He was held in a warehouse in Bani Walid, Libya, with fourteen other men in the same situation. He tried to run away twice and was sold three times before he was able to go back to Nigeria as a free man. Iabarot told *Time* magazine, "It was as if we weren't human."[55]

Over the past five years, an estimated 650,000 men and women have crossed the Sahara Desert in search of a better life in Europe. Almost all migration paths lead through Libya. Many refugee advocates and policy analysts agree that any attempt to alleviate the refugee crisis needs to address the lawlessness, kidnapping, forced prostitution, torture, and slavery that is happening in Libya. Julien Raikman, the Doctors Without Borders mission head in Libya, argues that refugees should not be taken back to Libya when they are intercepted in the Mediterranean Sea. In an interview with BBC, he articulated his confusion about why refugees are being sent back to Libya when they are apprehended at sea. He said, "This is what we don't understand. We say that [Libya] is not a port of safety."[56]

Protecting Child Refugees

The situation for refugees navigating through Libya is fraught with danger, and even more so for unaccompanied children. Identifying and protecting unaccompanied children is paramount to addressing the refugee crisis. The United Nations Children's Fund reports that in 2018, 42 percent (12,700) of migrant children arrived in Europe unaccompanied by an adult. Some of them began their voyage alone. Some had lost their parents to war in their home countries. Others lost them on the voyage to safety.

Among the unaccompanied children were Kedija and Yonas. Fifteen-year-old Kedija and her twelve-year-old brother, Yonas, fled Eritrea on their own. In 2010 their mother was forced to flee persecution and did not want to bring her young children on the dangerous journey, so she opted to leave them in the care of their grandparents. Five years later, the situation in Eritrea worsened, and Kedija and Yonas were forced to flee alone. They lived for some time in an Ethiopian refugee camp before being kidnapped at the Sudanese-Libyan border, held for ransom, and repeatedly sold from one smuggler to another. Eventually, they made their way onto a vessel to cross the Mediterranean Sea in hopes of making it to Europe and joining their mother in Switzerland. Unfortunately for them, the boat was rerouted back to Libya, where they were forced to stay at a detention center. With a lot of luck, their mother's perseverance in searching for her children, and help from the UNHCR in Libya,

A surprising number of refugees are unaccompanied minor children. These three young boys from Myanmar were photographed in a refugee camp in Thailand.

Kedija and Yonas were located and reunited with their mother. Their mother says, "Despite being separated for more than eight years, I never lost hope of being reunited with my kids again."[57]

The UNHCR explains that unaccompanied children are among the most vulnerable to kidnappers and human smugglers. Unaccompanied children are often sexually exploited as a way for smugglers to earn money. The UNHCR argues that unaccompanied children must be quickly identified at borders and migration centers so that they can be protected immediately by trained immigration officials. The UNHCR further calls for an end to the detainment of children for immigration purposes. To that end, the European Union Agency for Fundamental Rights states that it has been working with other partners to improve refugee children's support services since April 2016.

> **VIEWPOINT**
>
> ## The United States Should Support the Global Compact on Refugees
>
> Amina Mohammed, deputy secretary-general of the UN, holds out hope that the United States will reconsider its opposition to the Global Compact on Refugees. She believes that the compact provides an opportunity for all nations to work together and do their part in addressing the global refugee crisis.
>
> In recent years, we have seen a contagion of closed borders, contrary to international refugee and human rights law. Millions of refugees are facing years in exile, or risking their lives on dangerous journeys to an uncertain future.
>
> That is why this Global Compact is such an important step. It is a global commitment to step up and shoulder our responsibilities towards refugees; to find solutions that respect their human rights; to provide them with hope; and to recognize the legal responsibility to protect and support them.
>
> Amina Mohammed, "Deputy Secretary-General's Remarks to Mark the Adoption of the Global Compact on Refugees," United Nations, December 17, 2018. www.un.org.

Fixing Europe's Hotspots

Europe has been experiencing the bulk of the world's refugee arrivals. In order to address the dramatic increase of refugees coming to Europe by sea, the European Commission's European Agenda on Migration instituted the hotspot approach in April 2015. Hotspots are facilities in Greece and Italy established to identify and register refugees and migrants arriving by sea. In 2019 there were four in Italy and five in Greece.

The problem with hotspots is overcrowding and insufficient resources. In particular, Moria, on the Greek Island of Lesbos, is supposed to host three thousand asylum seekers, but in 2019 it housed thirteen thousand. Electra Petracou from the University of the Aegean argues, "Asylum Seekers in Moria Hot Spot are forced to live in inadequate and insecure living conditions and

VIEWPOINT

The United States Should Not Support the Global Compact on Refugees

Kelley Currie, US ambassador to the UN, voted against the Global Compact on Refugees. She agrees that action is needed to alleviate the refugee crisis but argues that parts of the compact go against US interests. Specifically, she opposes limiting the time that asylum seekers can be in detention and giving the UN decision-making authority in refugee resettlement matters.

> The United States has been a strong historical supporter of the work of the Office of the UN High Commissioner for Refugees to alleviate suffering, provide protection, and respect the dignity of refugees, internally displaced persons, stateless persons, and other persons of concern.
>
> However, we regret that the resolution before us today contains elements that run directly counter to my government's sovereign interests.
>
> We also have serious concerns with . . . alternatives to detention and the "need" to limit the detention of asylum seekers. We will detain and prosecute those who enter U.S. territory illegally, consistent with our domestic immigration laws and our international interests.

Kelley Currie, "Explanation of Vote in a Meeting of the Third Committee on a UNHCR Omnibus Resolution," United States Mission to the United Nations, November 13, 2018. https://usun.usmission.gov.

---

insufficient hygiene facilities. They suffer from both a lack of security and health care provision, which raises serious protection concerns."[58] Critics of the hotspot approach suggest that rather than housing refugees in a few overcrowded settlements, the European Union should work toward more international collaboration on quicker resettlements and integration. Others suggest that the hotspot approach is sufficient but needs more resources to speed up the application process and improve living conditions for refugees in camps and detention centers.

Global Obligations

One of the biggest concerns, aside from those related to security and living conditions, is the massive population of people who are waiting for refugee resettlement. There are nearly 26 million refugees worldwide, but not even one hundred thousand of them were resettled last year. In 2018 only one of every five hundred of the world's refugees were resettled. Many of the refugees waiting at camps do not have access to education, employment, or health care. Their lives are on hold while a collection of governing bodies decide their fate. Many are left to wonder (in some cases for years) whether they will be sent back to their country or granted refugee status, and if the latter, which country will take them in.

The UNHCR recognizes these problems and is working to alleviate the global refugee crisis. The UNHCR's Global Compact on Refugees, presented to the General Assembly in 2018, is an effort toward international cooperation for a global solution. In a

The UNHCR's Global Compact on Refugees seeks to enhance refugees' self-reliance, among other goals. In this camp in Kenya, a refugee practices tailoring to enhance her job skills.

report to the General Assembly, the compact's stated purpose is "to strengthen the international response to large movements of refugees and protracted refugee situations. It builds on existing international law and standards, including the 1951 Refugee Convention and human rights treaties, and seeks to better define cooperation to share responsibilities."[59]

The compact has four main objectives. First, it aims to ease the pressures on host countries. Eighty-five percent of refugees are hosted in developing countries. In Jordan one of eleven residents is a refugee, and in 2016 it cost Jordan about 25 percent of its annual budget to host refugees. Second, the compact intends to enhance refugee self-reliance, thereby improving their life circumstances and reducing costs to host nations. Next, it mentions expanding access to third-country solutions. This means that the countries not hosting the refugees in camps would create safe pathways for the refugees to go there. Finally, it aims to support conditions in countries of origin for return in safety and dignity.

Will Objectives Become Reality?

While the compact has broad objectives, many people are wondering what needs to be done to make those objectives a reality. For example, everyone—host nations and refugees alike—would like for refugees to be more self-reliant, but there is no agreement on what specifically needs to happen to make that possible. Critics also question whether the goal of third-country solutions is realistic, given the current anti-immigration rhetoric among politicians in the United States and Europe. Kemal Kirişci, a senior fellow at the Brookings Institution, writes, "The rise of populism and anti-immigration politics in Europe and the United States make the prospects for expanding access to third-country solutions politically challenging, at least in the near term."[60] In order to make the objectives of the Global Compact on Refugees a reality, European nations and the United States would need to substantially increase their refugee resettlement numbers or at least be willing to host refugees temporarily before they are resettled.

Refugee advocates suggest that global obligations to refugees should not be only about matters of the monetary costs and benefits of hosting refugees. Nations' policy debates over refugee resettlement should include humanitarian concerns—that is, the obligation to help people in a vulnerable and uncertain stage of their lives. David Miliband, chief executive officer of the International Rescue Committee, writes, "Refugees and displaced people have lost everything. But the refugee crisis is not just about 'them'; it is also about 'us'—what we, living in far greater comfort, stand for, and how we see our place in the world. It is a test of our character, not just our policies. Pass the test, and we rescue ourselves and our values as well as refugees and their lives."[61]

> "Refugees and displaced people have lost everything. But the refugee crisis is not just about 'them'; it is also about 'us'—what we, living in far greater comfort, stand for, and how we see our place in the world."[61]
>
> —David Miliband, chief executive officer of the International Rescue Committee

SOURCE NOTES

Introduction: A Global Crisis
1. Quoted in Save the Children, "Sana and Her Sisters: Leaving Syria," 2019. www.savethechildren.org.
2. Raea Rasmussen and Jacob Poushter, "People Around the World Express More Support for Taking In Refugees than Immigrants," Pew Research Center, August 9, 2019. www.pewresearch.org.

Chapter One: Who Are the Refugees?
3. Malala Yousafzai, *We Are Displaced: My Journey and Stories from Refugee Girls Around the World*. New York: Little, Brown, 2019, pp. 11–12.
4. Yousafzai, *We Are Displaced*, p. 3.
5. David Miliband, *Rescue: Refugees and the Political Crisis of Our Time*. New York: Simon and Schuster, 2017, p. 40.
6. Quoted in UNHCR Emergency Handbook, "Refugee Definition." https://emergency.unhcr.org.
7. Ishmael Beah, *A Long Way Gone: Memoirs of a Boy Soldier*. New York: Crichton, 2007, p. 199.
8. Quoted in Marion Hart, "After Two Years in Limbo, Rohingya Children Crave the Chance to Learn," UNICEF, August 26, 2019. www.unicefusa.org.
9. UNHCR, "Convention and Protocol Relating to the Status of Refugees." www.unhcr.org.
10. Quoted in Lily Rothman, "This Was President Truman's Powerful Message on Why the U.S. Should Help Refugees," *Time*, June 20, 2018. https://time.com.
11. António Guterres, "Remarks by António Guterres, United Nations High Commissioner for Refugees," UNHCR, October 28, 2014. www.unhcr.org.
12. Quoted in UNICEF, *Harrowing Journeys: Children and Youth on the Move Across the Mediterranean Sea, at Risk of Trafficking and Exploitation*. New York: UNICEF, 2017. www.unicef.org.

Chapter Two: The Perilous Journey

13. Hannah Wallace Bowman, "Your Spring Update from Refugee Rescue," Global Giving, May 15, 2019. www.globalgiving.org.
14. Quoted in Melissa Fleming, *A Hope More Powerful than the Sea: The Journey of Doaa Al Zamel*. New York: Flatiron, 2017, p. 192.
15. Quoted in Fleming, *A Hope More Powerful than the Sea*, p. 196.
16. UNHCR, *Desperate Journeys*. Geneva: UNHCR, 2019. www.unhcr.org.
17. Quoted in Yousafzai, *We Are Displaced*, p. 74.
18. Minority Rights Group International, "World Directory of Minorities and Indigenous Peoples—Myanmar/Burma: Muslims and Rohingya," 2017. www.refworld.org.
19. Quoted in Yousafzai, *We Are Displaced*, 2019, p. 171.
20. Quoted in UNHCR, *Desperate Journeys*.
21. Sandra Uwiringiyimana with Abigail Pesta, *How Dare the Sun Rise*. New York: Tegen, 2017, p. 71.
22. Claudia Martinez Mansell, "How to Navigate a Refugee Settlement," *Places Journal*, April 2016. https://placesjournal.org.
23. Quoted in Monica Costa Riba, "Women Face Daily Dangers in Greek Refugee Camps," Amnesty International, October 5, 2018 www.amnesty.org.
24. Barbie Latza Nadeau, "Migrants Are More Profitable than Drugs," *The Guardian* (Manchester), February 1, 2018. www.theguardian.com.

Chapter Three: Hurdles and Outcomes for Refugee Status

25. Quoted in BBC, "Rahaf Mohammad: Saudi Teen Says 'Women Treated like Slaves,'" January 15, 2019. www.bbc.com.
26. Quoted in Zamira Rahim, "Rahaf Mohammed al-Qunun: Saudi Teen Vows to Fight for Women's Rights Despite Facing 'Multiple' Threats," *The Independent* (London), January 16, 2019. www.independent.co.uk.

27. Quoted in Jack Herrara, "The Definition of Refugee Is Out-of-Date. And It's Leaving People Behind," *Pacific Standard*, June 27, 2019. https://psmag.com.
28. Uwiringiyimana with Pesta, *How Dare the Sun Rise*, pp. 98–100.
29. Quoted in Maria Sacchetti, "Victims of Domestic Abuse and Gang Violence Generally Won't Qualify for Asylum," *Washington Post*, June 11, 2018. www.washingtonpost.com.
30. Quoted in Lucy Perkins, "A New Approach to Refugees: Pay Them to Go Home," *All Things Considered*, NPR, January 13, 2018. www.npr.org.
31. US Citizenship and Immigration Services, "Refugees," October 24, 2017. www.uscis.gov.
32. Quoted in Aamna Mohdin and Ana Campoy, "Nearly 90% of People Pass the 'Credible Fear' Test for Refugees," *Quartz*, August 2, 2018. https://qz.com.
33. Dina Nayeri, "Waiting Is a Boot on Your Neck: How Refugees Summon Joy and Why They Hide It from Us," *Time*, September 17, 2019. https://time.com.
34. Quoted in Allyson Chiu, "Stunning in Ugliness and Tone: Trump Denounced for Attacking Somali Refugees in Minnesota," *Washington Post*, October 11, 2019. www.washingtonpost.com.
35. Uwiringiyimana with Pesta, *How Dare the Sun Rise*, 2017, p. 112.
36. Quoted in Abigail Pesta, "Life After Death: Teen Survivor of a Bloody Massacre Lives to Tell," *Daily Beast*, July 13, 2017. www.thedailybeast.com.

Chapter Four: The US Response

37. Quoted in Maegan Vazquez and Betsy Klein, "Trump Targets Somali Refugees During Minnesota Rally," CNN, October 11, 2019. www.cnn.com.
38. Quoted in Amanda Taub and Max Fisher, "Trump's Refugee Cuts Threaten Deep Consequences at Home and Abroad," *New York Times*, September 11, 2019. www.nytimes.com.

39. Quoted in *The Guardian* (Manchester), "Full Transcript of Trump's Phone Call with Australian Prime Minister Malcolm Turnbull," August 3, 2017. www.theguardian.com.
40. Quoted in Griff Witte, "They're the Refugees That Trump Tried to Stop but Now They're Here and They're Becoming Americans," *Washington Post*, October 12, 2019. www.washingtonpost.com.
41. Quoted in *The Guardian* (Manchester), "Full Transcript of Trump's Phone Call with Australian Prime Minister Malcolm Turnbull."
42. Matthew Levitt, "Trump's Travel Ban Might Be Legal, but It's Bad Policy," *Foreign Policy*, April 25, 2018. https://foreignpolicy.com.
43. Quoted in Tucker Higgins, "Supreme Court Rules That Trump's Travel Ban Is Constitutional," CNBC, June 26, 2018. www.cnbc.com.
44. Quoted in AP News, "Book Says Trump Adviser Spoke Dismissively About Refugees," January 28, 2019. www.apnews.com.
45. Quoted in Eileen Sullivan, "What Is the Refugee Program and Why Does the Trump Administration Want to Make Cuts?," *New York Times*, September 6, 2019. www.nytimes.com.
46. Quoted in Julie Hirschfeld Davis and Somini Sengupta, "Trump Administration Rejects Study Showing Positive Impact of Refugees," *New York Times*, September 18, 2017. www.nytimes.com.
47. Quoted in Davis and Sengupta, "Trump Administration Rejects Study Showing Positive Impact of Refugees."
48. Quoted in Ted Hesson, "Trump Administration Nearly Halves Refugee Cap for Coming Year," Politico, September 26, 2019. www.politico.com.

Chapter Five: In Search of a Global Solution

49. Quoted in New Humanitarian, "An Open Secret: Refugee Push-Backs Across the Turkey-Greece Border," October 8, 2018. www.thenewhumanitarian.org.

50. Quoted in New Humanitarian, "An Open Secret."
51. Quoted in New Humanitarian, "An Open Secret."
52. United Nations Office on Drugs and Crime, "Prosecuting Human Traffickers," 2019. www.unodc.org.
53. United Nations Office on Drugs and Crime, "Prosecuting Human Traffickers."
54. Deutsche Welle, "Widespread Torture and Rape Documented in Libya's Refugee Camps," March 26, 2019. www.dw.com.
55. Quoted in Aryn Baker, "Inside the Modern Slave Trade Trapping African Migrants," *Time*, March 14, 2019. https://time.com.
56. Quoted in Rana Jawad, "Migrant Crisis: Self-Immolation Exposes UN Failures in Libya," BBC, July 31, 2019. www.bbc.com.
57. Quoted in UNHCR, *Desperate Journeys*.
58. Quoted in FFM Online, "The 'Hotspot' Approach Is Not the Solution," 2019. https://ffm-online.org.
59. United Nations, "Refugees and Migrants: Global Compact on Refugees," 2019. https://refugeesmigrants.un.org.
60. Kemal Kirişci, "How to Make Concrete Progress on the Global Compact on Refugees," Brookings Institution, June 7, 2019. www.brookings.edu.
61. Miliband, *Rescue*, p. 6.

ORGANIZATIONS AND WEBSITES

European Council on Refugees and Exiles (ECRE)
—www.ecre.org

The ECRE's website explains the council's mission and provides links to its work protecting and advancing refugee rights in the realms of litigation, policy research, advocacy, and communication.

International Rescue Committee (IRC)—www.rescue.org

The IRC's main website describes what the organization does and provides links to personal refugee stories and press updates.

Migration Policy Institute (MPI)—www.migrationpolicy.org

The MPI's website offers links to articles and recent research on the impacts of refugee policy, migration patterns, and facts and data about immigrants in the United States.

Refugee Council USA (RCUSA)—www.rcusa.org

The RCUSA's website offers information and statistics on refugees arriving in the United States, as well as information about refugee resettlement and how to get involved.

United Nations High Commissioner for Refugees (UNHCR)
—www.unhcr.org

The UNHCR's main website provides current news on the global refugee situation. There are also links to information about what the UNHCR is doing around the world and how interested people can get involved.

US Citizenship and Immigration Services (USCIS)
—www.uscis.gov

The USCIS refugee website provides the legal definition of *refugee*, procedural information, and links to current news and alerts.

US Office of Refugee Resettlement (ORR)
—www.acf.hhs.gov/orr

The ORR's website explains the ORR's mandate and provides information on its history and links detailing the specific ways in which it helps refugees resettle in the United States.

FOR FURTHER RESEARCH

Books

Melissa Fleming, *A Hope More Powerful than the Sea: The Journey of Doaa Al Zamel*. New York: Flatiron, 2017.

Jim Gallagher, *Refugees and Asylum*. San Diego, CA: ReferencePoint, 2020.

Stuart A. Kallen, *Crisis on the Border: Refugees and Undocumented Immigrants*. San Diego, CA: ReferencePoint, 2020.

Linda Barrett Osbourne, *This Land Is Our Land: A History of American Immigration*. New York: Abrams Books for Young Readers, 2016.

Sandra Uwiringiyimana with Abigail Pesta, *How Dare the Sun Rise*. New York: Tegen, 2017.

Malala Yousafzai, *We Are Displaced: My Journey and Stories from Refugee Girls Around the World*. New York: Little, Brown, 2019.

Internet Sources

Michael D. Shear and Zolan Kanno-Youngs, "Trump Slashes Refugee Cap to 18,000, Curtailing U.S. Role as Haven," *New York Times*, September 26, 2019. www.nytimes.com.

UNHCR, *Desperate Journeys*. Geneva: UNHCR, 2019. www.unhcr.org.

UNHCR, "Figures at a Glance," 2019. www.unhcr.org.

UNHCR, "Syria Refugee Crisis," 2019. www.unhcr.org.

UNHCR, "U.S. Resettlement Facts," 2019. www.unhcr.org.

United Nations Population Fund, "A Call to Protect Women and Girls on the Move," ReliefWeb, October 8, 2018. https://reliefweb.int.

INDEX

Note: Boldface page numbers indicate illustrations.

Abdelwahab, Mahmoud, 35–36
Adam, Abdisalam, 41
Afghanistan, 26
Alarm Phone, 21–22
Albright, Madeleine, 13
Al Zamel, Doaa, 22
Ash, Nazanin, 44
asylum
  grounds for, 33, 34, 37–38
  terrorist attacks by seekers of, in Europe, 46
  UNHCR and, 37
  in United States
    process, 40
    seekers on border with Mexico, 48, 50–52, **51**
Ataie, Ali Reza, 44–46
Australia, 44, 45

Bach, Thomas, 35
Beah, Ishmael, 14
Bentiu, South Sudan, 28
Bourj Al Shamali (refugee camp in Lebanon), 27–29
boy soldiers, 14

Canada, 32
Çapan, Murat, 54
Cara di Mineo camp (Sicily), 30
Cato Institute, 46
children
  arriving in Europe unaccompanied by adult (2018), 58
  conditions faced by unaccompanied, 58–59
  number of refugees worldwide, 6
  percent of refugees worldwide, 19
  in refugee camps, 28–29
  sexual assault of unaccompanied, 59
  unaccompanied, from Myanmar, **59**
Convention Relating to the Status of Refugees (UN, 1951), 12, 16, 17
Cuccinelli, Ken, 52
Currie, Kelley, 61

Deutsche Welle (German-owned public broadcasting company), 57
displaced persons (DP) camps after World War II, 16, 17
Displaced Persons Act (US, 1948), 18
Dobbs, Leo, 54
Doctors Without Borders, 28, 55

Einstein, Albert, 13
English Channel, crossing, 26
Estefan, Gloria, 13

73

European Agenda on Migration (European Commission), 60
European Union Agency for Fundamental Rights, 59

Fleming, Melissa, 22

gendered violence. *See* women, dangers faced by
Global Compact on Refugees, **62**
   overview of, 62–63
   realism of objectives, 63–64
   United States and, 60, 61
Greece, 60–61
Guardian (British newspaper), 26, 30

Harrowing Journeys (United Nations Children's Fund), 19–20
Hellenic League for Human Rights, 54
Hesar, Ali, 44–46
Holocaust, 16, 17
hotspots, 60–61
Human Rights Watch, 32
human smugglers/human traffickers
   children and, 59
   deaths and, 22, 25
   experience described, 22–24
   laws outlawing and prosecuting, are needed, 54–55
   NGOs as aiding, 55–56

   ransoms, 25
   rape by, 25

Iabarot, Sunday, 57
immigrants, willingness of host countries to accept, 8
Internal Displacement Monitoring Centre, 14
internally displaced persons (IDPs)
   legal rights of, 13, 15
   number of Syrian, 18
   reasons for leaving homes, 14
   from South Sudan, 28
International Organization for Migration, 30, 40
International Rescue Committee, 13
Iraq, 35–36
Islam, 47–48
Israel, 35
Italy, 60

Jordan, 63
journeys
   from Afghanistan, 26
   dangers described, 6–7, 21
      attacks on boats, 22
      faced by unaccompanied children, 58–59
      faced by women, 25, **29**, 29–30
   deaths, 21, 25
   human smugglers, 23–24
   Libyan route, 25

Kirişci, Kemal, 63
Kizuka, Kennji, 33
K'naan, 13
Kunis, Mila, 13

Lebanon, 27–29
Levitt, Matthew, 48
Libya, 25, 57–58

Mansell, Claudia Martinez, 28–29
Martinez, Giron, 50–51
McAleenan, Kevin, 48
Mediterranean Sea, deaths while crossing, 21
migrant camps. *See* refugee camps
migrants, 15–16
Miliband, David, 12, 64
Miller, Stephen, 49
Minority Rights Group International, 24
Mohammed, Amina, 60
Mohammed, Jamal Abdelmaji Eisa, 35
Mohammed, Rahaf, 31–32, **32,** 33, 34
Muday, Muna, 39
Murdza, Katy, 38
Myanmar, persecution of Rohingya, **15,** 24–25

Nadeau, Barbie Latza, 30
national security, 39, 46–48, **47**
Nauru, refugee camps on, 45
Nayeri, Dina, 38

Nazism, 17
New York Times (newspaper), 49
Nigerian women, 30
nongovernmental organizations (NGOs), 28, 55–56, **56**

Obama, Barack, 44
Olympic Games, 35

Pakistan, Taliban policies and actions in, 10
Petracou, Electra, 60–61
Pew Research Center, 8, 47
Pouri, Ahmed, 38
prostitution, 30
Pupa, Michael, 16
pushbacks, 53–54

Raikman, Julien, 58
Reed, Jack, 49
Refugee Act (US, 1980), 39, 44
refugee camps, **15, 36**
  conditions in, 8, 62
    bathroom facilities, 28, 29–30
    in Libya, 57
    lines for food and water, 26–27, **27**
    on Nauru, 45
  cost of, 63
  hotspots as answer, 60–61
  for IDPs, 28
  permanent, 27–29

recreational activities in, 42
responsibility for security in, 29
Refugee Convention (UN, 1951), 12, 16, 17
Refugee Rescue, 21
refugees
  definition of, 12–13, 33
  famous, 13
  legal rights of, 16
  native countries of most, 18
  number worldwide, 6
  return to native countries, 35–36
  status as
    applying for, 37
    barriers to obtaining, 34–35
    criteria for, 38
    United States and, 37, 40
  from Turkey, 53–54
  during World War II, 17
Refugee Status Determination (RSD), 37
Refugee Whisperer, The, 38
resettlement
  debates about logistics of, 9
  largest host countries, 19, **19**
  public opinion about, 8
  rates
    in 2016, 9
    in 2018, 7–8, 9, 61–62
    countries with higher, than United States, 43
  September 11, 2001
    suspension of, by United States, 39
  Trump policy, 39
  in United States
    ceilings (2017–2020), 39
    decrease in number, 9
    economic effect, 43, 49–50
    process described, 40–42, **41**
    states with largest numbers of, 40
    Trump local refusal policy, 39
  after World War II, 17–18
Roberts, John, 48
Rohingya, persecution of, **15,** 24–25
Rosenthal, Bernice, 16
Rosenthal, Edward, 16

Save the Children, 55
Sessions, Jeff, 34
sex trafficking, 30
sexual assault
  of unaccompanied children, 59
  of women
    asylum and, 34
    in camps, 57
    culture of silence around, 34
    by intimate partners, 33
    by smugglers, 25
    trafficking, 30
Somalia, refugees from, 6, 13, 18, 39, 41
SOS Méditerranée, 56
South Sudan, refugees from, 6, 18, 28, 35

Sudan
  number of refugees from, 6, 18
  as refugee-hosting country, 19, **19,** 35
Syria
  conditions in, 6, 18
  refugees from, **7**
    as largest refugee population in world, 18
    number of, 6
    willingness to accept, 8, 47

Telling the Real Story information campaign (UNHCR), 25
terrorism, 39, 46–48, **47**
Time (magazine), 57
tourists and terrorism, 46
trafficking, 30
Truman, Harry, 17–18
Trump, Donald, **45,** 46
  changes in American resettlement policy
    cuts in admissions, 44
    effects of, 9
    states and cities allowed to veto refugee resettlements, 39
  community costs of resettlement, 43
  refusal to honor agreements made by Obama, 44
  travel ban on Muslims, 47–48
Turnbull, Malcolm, 44

Ungrateful Refugee, The: What Immigrants Never Tell You (Nayeri), 38
United Nations Children's Fund, 19–20, 58
United Nations High Commissioner for Refugees (UNHCR)
  asylum and, 37
  calls for end to pushbacks, 54
  creation of, 17
  estimate of percent of refugees settled in 2018, 7–8
  Global Compact on Refugees, **62**
    overview of, 62–63
    realism of objectives, 63–64
    United States and, 60, 61
  on journeys, 22
  number of deaths on Mediterranean Sea per arrival, 55
  number of internally displaced Syrians, 18
  number of people in refugee camps in Libya, 57
  number of refugees in 2018, 12
  number of Syrian refugees, 6
  protection of children and end to detainment of called for, 59
  refugee status and, 37
  travel through Libya, 25

United Nations Office on Drugs and Crime (UNODC), 55
United States
  asylum seekers
    on border with Mexico, 48, 50–52, **51**
    process for, 40
  countries with higher resettlement rates, 43
  deaths crossing border with Mexico, 25
  Department of Health and Human Services (HHS), 49–50
  Displaced Persons Act, 18
  famous refugees in, 13
  Global Compact on Refugees and, 60, 61
  presidents honoring agreements made by predecessors, 44
  processing of refugee claims, 35
  public opinion about accepting refugees from Syria, 47
  Refugee Convention and, 17
  refugee status, 37, 40
  resettlement in
    ceilings (2017–2020), 39
    decrease in number, 9
    economic effect, 43, 49–50
    process described, 40–42, **41**
  states with largest numbers of, 40
  after World War II, 17–18
  September 11, 2001
    suspension of refugee resettlements, 39
  traditionally safe haven for refugees, 49
  See also Trump, Donald
UN Women, 33–34
Uwiringiyimana, Sandra, 26–27, 34, 41–42

women, dangers faced by
  nonsexual violence against
    asylum and, 33, 34
    by families, 31–32, **32**
    by intimate partners, 33–34
  in refugee camps, 29–30
  sexual assault, 57
    asylum and, 34
    culture of silence around, 34
    by intimate partners, 33
    by smugglers, 25
  trafficking, 30
World Health Organization, 15
World Relief, 39
World War II, 16, 17

Yemen, 22–23
Yousafzai, Malala, 10–12, **11**, 23–24

PICTURE CREDITS

Cover: answer5/Shutterstock

7: Istan Csak/Shutterstock.com
11: JStone/Shutterstock.com
15: Hafiz Johari/Shutterstock.com
19: Maury Aaseng
23: Nicolas Economou/Shutterstock.com
27: Adjin Kamber/Shutterstock.com
29: Ververidis Vasilis/Shutterstock.com
32: Associated Press
36: Orlok/Shutterstock.com
41: Associated Press
45: Leah Mills/Reuters/Newscom
47: Michal Kappeler/dpa/picture-alliance/Newscom
51: Vic Hinterlang/Shutterstock.com
56: Gerard Bottino/Shutterstock.com
59: Seipoe/Shutterstock.com
62: Adriana Mahdalova/Shutterstock.com

ABOUT THE AUTHOR

Stephanie Lundquist-Arora has master's degrees in political science and public administration. She helped organize and facilitate Amnesty International London's Gender and Refugee Conference. As a Presidential Management Fellow for the US Department of Justice Criminal Division, she analyzed data on emerging trends relating to immigration prosecutions in southwestern border districts. When not writing, Lundquist-Arora likes traveling with her family, jogging, learning jujitsu, reading, and trying new foods.